EVERYDAY *storyteller*

33 PRACTICAL IDEAS FROM REAL WORLD SCRAPBOOKERS

The Magic of Everyday

Everyday: encountered or used routinely or typically; ordinary.

My passion is helping people turn stories into scrapbook pages and find ease in the start-to-finish journey. I love connecting memory keepers with processes and techniques that open the doors to deeper meaning and greater freedom in scrapbook projects.

For me, this most often means getting back-to-basics and embracing simple, ordinary approaches that really work. Everyday Storyteller is a celebration of my philosophy of real-world scrapbooking. I reached out to members of our community to assist me in sharing a collection of the best practical ideas for paper, digital and hybrid scrapbookers alike.

From framing a moment in your mind's eye to expressing your heart on the page, this book offers tips and tricks you can use right now in your memory keeping. I want to help you see the magic of scrapbooking not only in your everyday life, but in the essential techniques that help get pages finished. And while there is plenty of visual inspiration in this book, my mission was to build a publication as truly useful to you as it is beautiful.

I would first like to thank my husband for helping me find laughter in the everyday and my daughter for being my daily reminder that anything is possible. Bringing this book to fruition was truly a team effort. Without Lynnette and Neisha by my side, this book wouldn't exist. The contributors deserve the most credit, however, for crafting incredible projects and breaking them down into bite-sized tips for you. I hope you will utilize these storytelling ideas to make your everyday extraordinary.

Jennifer S. Wilson

JENNIFER S. WILSON

Contents

The Magic of Everyday............. 03
JENNIFER S. WILSON

Why Storytelling Matters............. 06
KATIE CLEMONS

Capturing Moments

Celebrate Everyday Life with Your
Scrapbooking............................. 10
CRYSTAL LIVESAY

Finding Great Light for
Photographing Great Memories..... 12
KATRINA KENNEDY

Celebrating Everyday Moments
with Instant Photography............. 14
JESSICA SPRAGUE

Capturing Memories, Not Portraits... 16
AMANDA PADGETT

Outside-the-Box Approaches for
Regular Journaling..................... 18
ANGIE LUCAS

Journaling the Way You Think........ 20
BETSY SAMMARCO

Documenting Everyday Dialogue... 22
SARA GLEASON

Prepare for Scrapbooking Using an
iPad and the Apple iPhoto App 24
RENEE PEARSON

Telling Stories

Looking Forward and Back to
Create Meaningful Stories................ 28
KRISTIN RUTTEN

Four Tips for Prioritizing Creativity
Every Day.................................. 30
CHERYL ASHCRAFT

Tips for Easy Guilt-Free
Scrapbooking............................. 32
TRACI REED

Enhance Your Memory Keeping
with Social Media........................ 34
AMBER RIES

Taking Stories from Blog to Page... 36
CHRISTINE NEWMAN

Fast and Easy Journaling with
Lists... 38
ELLE PRICE

Journaling from the Heart............. 40
HEATHER PRINS

Use Little Memories to Celebrate
Big Stories................................. 42
JENNIFER S. WILSON

Inexpensive Details for Heartfelt
Stories...................................... 44
BY CD MUCKOSKY

Creating Memories

Defining Your Scrapbooking Style Recipe.................. 48
MELISSA STINSON

Designing Successful Page Layouts with a Sketchbook.............. 50
TIFFANY TILLMAN

Improvisational Scrapbooking with Sketches.................. 52
JENN SMITH-SLOANE

Two Simple Shortcuts for Photo Arrangement.................. 54
PAULA GILARDE

Create a Simple Vintage Collage In Three Steps 56
NANCY NALLY

Combine Your Go-To Foundations for Quick, Richly Layered Pages......... 58
DEBBIE HODGE

Simple Techniques for Visual Complexity.................. 60
ANNA ASPNES

Create Cohesive Layouts with Repetition.................. 62
CINDY LIEBEL

Using Digital Papers and Elements on Traditional Layouts.................. 64
ROBYN MEIEROTTO

Easy Scrapbook Lettering with Alphabet Stamps.................. 66
MICHELLE HERNANDEZ

Three Creative Ways to Use Stencils on Your Scrapbook Pages.................. 68
AMY KINGSFORD

Wet Media: Three Easy Techniques for Layouts.................. 70
ASHLI OLIVER

Documenting Real Life with Souvenirs and Ephemera.................. 72
AMY TAN

Four Techniques for Building a Cohesive Mini Book.................. 74
ELISE CRIPE

Tracking Your Scrapbook Supplies with Spreadsheets 76
LAUREN REID

EVERYDAY storyteller

Jennifer S. Wilson
EDITOR

Lynnette Penacho
DESIGNER

Neisha Sykes
COPY EDITOR

COPYRIGHT © 2012 CREATE MORE MEDIA. ALL RIGHTS RESERVED.

COVER PHOTO BY ROBYN MEIEROTTO.

EVERYDAY STORYTELLER • 5

Why Storytelling Matters

by Katie Clemons

The stories of life are the heart of scrapbooking.

The moments, the people and the memories are what move us to create our pages and pause to celebrate the good stuff of life. While new products and embellishments can make our pages look beautiful, they can also distract us from capturing this heart of life.

We start worrying that our pages won't look the way we think they should. We lock up, fall behind and miss documenting the good stuff in life all because of our fear of imperfection. That's where a focus on words instead of decorative stuff comes in.

Today, I want you to say yes to telling more stories on your pages. In fact, try this: think of your layout not as a scrapbook page, but a decorated journal entry.

Journaling the stories and adventures of my family's life makes me so much more aware of the day-to-day. It teaches me to pay closer attention to life and to celebrate stories. It teaches me gratitude. And best of all, approaching scrapbooking like a journal helps me tell those stories that I was too intimidated to tell on 12x12-inch pages!

When you focus on the story on your pages instead of the stuff on your pages, you'll find yourself okay with imperfect penmanship. You'll find yourself okay with an imperfect layout. You'll be okay with not having the most beautiful or latest scrapbooking embellishments.

Take the picture on the previous page for instance. All I used was a writing prompt journal from my shop, www.gadanke.com, a red pen, one photo and a scrap of red- and white-striped paper.

I'm embracing my page's imperfection. After all, it captures an imperfect day of blizzards and canceled flights. Isn't everything about our lives imperfect? And isn't that okay? Maybe even beautiful?

I'd rather document those imperfect days then never have my stories told. Below is another page from later in that same journal.

I've got most of the basics: photo, title, embellishments. But where's the story? Why was this impromptu picture snapped? Who snapped it? Does it mean anything? Who's the baby? Does it really matter?

Story makes it matter.

As we make story-keeping a habit, the little pieces of story start to build. All of a sudden, it isn't just capturing moments. It's capturing life.

Take my journal for example. (Yes, I call it a *journal*, not a *scrapbook* to make sure I'm keeping true to story.) Early in my journal, I'm sharing the story of a blizzard that almost prevented us from returning to the United States for Christmas. Then, there are stories of arriving at my parents' house, more and more people coming for the holidays, traditions happening... and best of all, meeting our new niece on the page below.

Was it the best Christmas ever? Who knows. I'm just so thankful my book has become a celebration of people and moments, not a struggle over pretty embellishments (that I probably wouldn't have finished!). Today, when our family flips through the pages of this journal rich with bits of story, we are transported back to each of those moments that we would have forgotten about.

Are you ready to embrace imperfection? To say yes to more story?

Capturing Moments

Storytelling begins with words and photos. Through simple documentation we may celebrate the unique lens with which we view the world. To truly grasp a moment however, we must pause, watch, and listen.

Celebrate Everyday Life with Your Scrapbooking
by Crystal Livesay

Most scrapbookers are great at documenting birthdays, baby's first steps and soccer championships. However, we often neglect to tell our own stories. Occasionally, we might scrap an anniversary or some other big moment, but what about the little details of our everyday lives? What about your own daily routine?

What did you do for breakfast? How did you spend your afternoon? Did you go for that run in the evening? There are lots of things about ourselves that we think are not worth telling, but these things are who we are! These are the things our kids will remember.

For example, I remember when I was a kid, every time we got in the car my mom would play John Mellencamp. From the time I was six years old I could sing along and even had a favorite John Mellencamp song. To this day, every time I hear him, I think of being in the car with my mom singing and just being together. It's an awesome feeling! So, keep your camera or phone with you and take photos throughout your day and get those daily happenings recorded. There are lots of different ways you can keep notes, too, either digitally with programs like Oh Life! or traditionally with a journal or even scraps of paper. It's so easy! It takes only a few seconds to snap a shot and a few minutes more at the end of the day to record what you did.

I have also found that by taking mundane types of photos, it improves my photography and makes me take more creative shots. Daily memory keeping helps me grow and I am so grateful for that. I bet when your kids look back at your everyday photos they will giggle and reminisce about the things they loved about you!

How to Get Started Documenting Daily Life

So, how should your get started documenting your daily life? Begin first thing in the morning and go from there. Here's a look at my day as I documented it using Instagram to show you just how easy it can be to record your everyday.

1 Morning Routine
What is the first thing you do in the morning? Take the time to document the details of your morning routine.

2 Focus on the Details
Even little things like getting dressed or picking out accessories are fun to record. I know that my daughter loves looking at my jewelry and does it daily. We will always remember that!

3 Capture Your Day
Don't forget to include some of the things you like to do on a particular day. On Sundays, I always work on my Project Life.

4 Bedtime Routine
I always end my day in the same way: tucking the kids in and reading from my massive pile of books. Usually, I end up passing out while making my way through the pile!

Finding Great Light for Photographing Great Memories

by Katrina Kennedy

Great photos are the foundation of my favorite scrapbook pages. I love a photo that grabs my attention, shouts, "Look at me!" and pulls me into its details. How do I create those kinds photos for my everyday storytelling? I start my memory keeping by finding amazing light.

1 Scout the Light

I work to anticipate good lighting. If I know we are going somewhere that has amazing light, the camera comes with me. I keep a mental collection of all the great-light locations I know. With that mental list, I know when I'm really going to want my camera and when I can leave it at home because I won't love the photos that I take.

Photographing other people's events and at their homes can be a little trickier. I'll take my camera, but even then I'm looking for light. Watching the light gives me an idea of exactly when to pick up the camera and when to just enjoy the time with my family.

2 Look for Good Light

Finding the right light can make or break a photo. Look for these great light sources:

- Even light. Even light is not dappled and there are no hot spots. Great even light makes eyes sparkle and skin shine.
- Large catch lights. Those beautiful, white reflections in someone's eyes are called catch lights. They make a person's face have life and personality. Catch lights often appear simply by moving a few inches to one side or another.
- Indirect light. I want windows and light sources that don't create harsh shadows under eyes. I look for open, shady spots or an overcast day.

Top Tips for Great Light in your Photographs

Put Your Back to the Light
When your back is to your light source, the best light falls on your subject. You know your light source is too bright and too high when your subject is squinting or has gigantic shadows under their eyes.

Step Around
Move around your subject to see how the light changes. I try to do this in stealth mode when possible. Watch the catch lights and the overall quality of the light on your subject.

Pick Your Seat
In restaurants I always try to seat myself with my back to the windows. If my back is to the windows then beautiful light comes in and covers whomever I'm with.

Make Suggestions
Birthday parties and family events can be a little tricky. Since I'm carrying the camera, sometimes I can give a little direction by asking the subject to move to better light. I want to avoid light from behind so I can see his face.

Move Things
If you have young children, place their toys and books in your best light locations. They will naturally move there to entertain themselves and you've got a memory ready to be captured!

Wait for Good Light
When the sun is low on the horizon, just after sunrise and just before sunset, you'll often find even, diffused, golden light. This is called the Golden Hour. Take advantage of this light to really make your photos pop.

Celebrating Everyday Moments with Instant Photography
by Jessica Sprague

"Wait, wait! Let me get a picture!" I say as I pull my camera from my purse or pocket. Snap. I spend a few seconds setting a filter that warms the photo and gives it a rounded-edge frame, type a quick caption and done. Another memory saved.

This camera is different. Rather than just saving onto a memory card, this photo has now been shared instantly with my friends and family through a web site and through Facebook and Twitter.

The camera I'm using in this scenario – which happens almost every day – is actually my phone. I use Instagram, a free app that lets me record my life's story in little four-inch square bits and pieces. And all are pre-framed, pre-filtered and perfect for including in my digital scrapbook and Project Life pages. I even have an Instagram feed on my blog to display my most recent snaps.

In general, I'm an okay photographer. I have taken my share of both incredible and not-so-incredible photos with my nice, big digital SLR camera. It still comes with me on special trips and occasions. But for the "Oh cute! Must record and share this!" slices of life, which happen so much more often than the big trips and events, my phone plus Instagram is my go-to camera. I think this is partly because when I hold my phone I am able to let go of my anxiety to get a great shot. I let it go and just snap the moment.

I think this method also helps me be able to forget some of the anxiety I feel to stay caught up with sharing things with friends and family. My SLR camera workflow involves getting photos off of the camera, editing and resizing them in Photoshop, adding in a frame, then uploading them to my blog or to Flickr. Nothing could be better for me than a quick click of the Instagram button, knowing I have saved my photo to my camera for later scrapbooking and also knowing that others have shared the moment with me right then. That sense of immediacy is wonderful since most of my friends and family live far from me.

My app of choice may change – heck, my camera of choice may change. But what I love about my life right now is the little everyday stuff. My kids. My home. My adventures in business and mommyhood, wifehood and lifehood. I love ordinary moments and making time stand still for a little while in a simple memory. Instagram is perfect for recording and sharing just such ordinary, extraordinary things.

CAPTURING MOMENTS • 15

Capturing Memories, Not Portraits
by Amanda Padgett

When looking through my own childhood photo albums, I don't look at the portraits and think, "Oh, that was a great day!" Nope. More often than not, I may have bad memories of that day. Instead, it is the pictures of me carrying a favorite stuffed animal or a playing a board game that bring back good memories and give me the warm-fuzzies. Now that I am the record-keeper of memories for my family, I try to pay attention and capture those sweet moments that my children, husband and I will look back on someday and smile. These are some of the approaches I use to document deeper stories and good memories in my photographs.

1. Record the Activity and the Result

My memories of my children and the memories they will have later are usually going to be of everyday happenings such as drawing a stickman for the first time. This is an activity done by almost every child, but ten years from now will I remember what that first stickman looked like?

2. Take the Focus Off the Subject

A good way to capture sweet memories and not portraits is to purposely *not* have the focus be on my child. Whether I use my mobile phone or my digital SLR, I choose the focal point, make it land on what my child or children are playing with or playing on and take the shot. I have a ton of pictures of my children. What I am striving to capture is the object of their enjoyment, the love for their doll or the ingenuity they used to create that complex spaceship.

3. Get Down on Their Level

Another easy way to capture the process or activity of my loved ones is involves changing my viewpoint. I move down lower so that the camera and I are on level with what they are playing with or making. Down low, the camera can catch their hands playing or creating. After they are through, I try to capture the final result of their activity, like the final Lego building or play-dough creature, from that same level. I make the result the subject.

The Picture Remembers

The photographs I've shared with you were taken because I was so tickled by the hard work my daughter did to create a home for her dolls. She was so creative and resourceful, but would I remember these moments ten years from now? Probably not. With pictures of her creations and of her playing with them, I can look back and the tenderness I was feeling when I watched her will come back. The picture remembers.

CAPTURING MOMENTS • 17

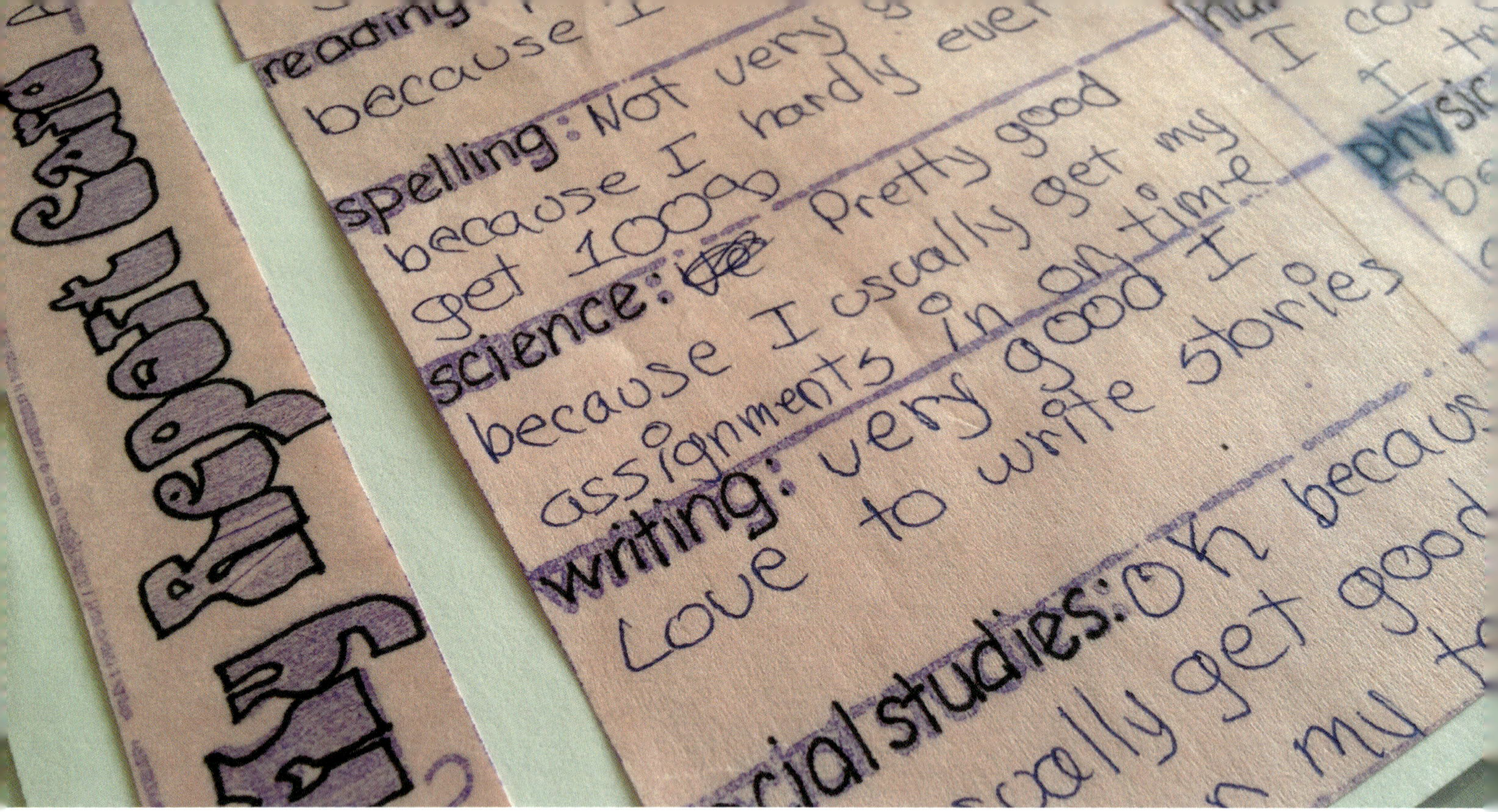

Outside-the-Box Approaches for Regular Journaling

by Angie Lucas

I've loved to write for as long as I can remember.

I have a school assignment from the third grade that proclaims, twice, how proud I was of my writing. And clearly, the fact that I kept that assignment shows that I was also destined to be a saver of memories.

At that young age I only knew of one way to write, one way to save memories and that was with a pencil. I couldn't even conceive of all the different options now available for storytellers. In 1984, who could have imagined that one day we'd be typing thoughts, notes and memories into cordless telephones that are small enough to carry in our pockets?

The obvious way to journal is chronologically. But it's not the only way. And I found the strict chronological approach was fraught with problems for me. Years ago, when I kept

just one journal at a time, I'd have a flash of inspiration and grab my journal to write about it then I'd notice that I was about nine months behind. Unless I felt like writing a marathon catch-up entry, I'd sigh and put the journal away.

Clearly, my journal-writing approach was not effective for me. So, I've opened myself up to a myriad of ways to save my stories. The biggest benefits of writing and journaling are the immediate insights and understanding that follow: the gratitude, the reminder to pay attention, the motivation to strive daily to live a life that's worth writing about.

Five Ways I Journal My Stories

1 Scrapbook Pages

My scrapbook pages are very story-based. I almost never create a layout that doesn't include at least a little bit of journaling on it. Like my journal-writing, I keep my scrapbooking pressure-free. I scrapbook whatever I want, whenever I want to.

2 Letters to My Daughter Journal

Ever since her first birthday, I've been writing Keira one letter per week. I fill one side of one page each week and I like how the limited space keeps me focused and brief. For the first year of her life, I kept a memory-a-day calendar for her, where I filled one square of a standard calendar with just one tiny thought about her each day.

3 Encyclopedia.doc

Inspired by the book *Encyclopedia of an Ordinary Life* by Amy Krouse Rosenthal, I have an ongoing word-processing document on my computer titled Encyclopedia.doc. When I have a random memory that I want to save, I simply add a new alphabetical topic to this document. These entries are always standalone memories, they're usually humorous and they're often half-finished thoughts that I plan to expand upon later. My favorite entry is "Things I Finally Understood When I Was Embarrassingly Old."

4 My Compliments Journal

I created a tiny, handmade notebook where I save the best, most sincere compliments I've received - the words that have made me feel like I've been truly seen for who I am or want to be. I turn to this little notebook when I need a reminder that I matter. My favorite entry, one I've had memorized since high school, came from my favorite English teacher on a letter of recommendation. She said, "Angie is very intelligent, but that's not the best thing about her. The best thing about her is her character."

5 Overheard Within These Walls

I've been keeping this notebook of family quotes for a few years now. When I hear something funny, insightful or truly memorable spoken within the walls of my home, I pull it out and capture the words while the memory is fresh. These quotes occasionally end up on scrapbook pages, but I like keeping this as a self-contained journal as well.

Journaling the Way You Think

by Betsy Sammarco

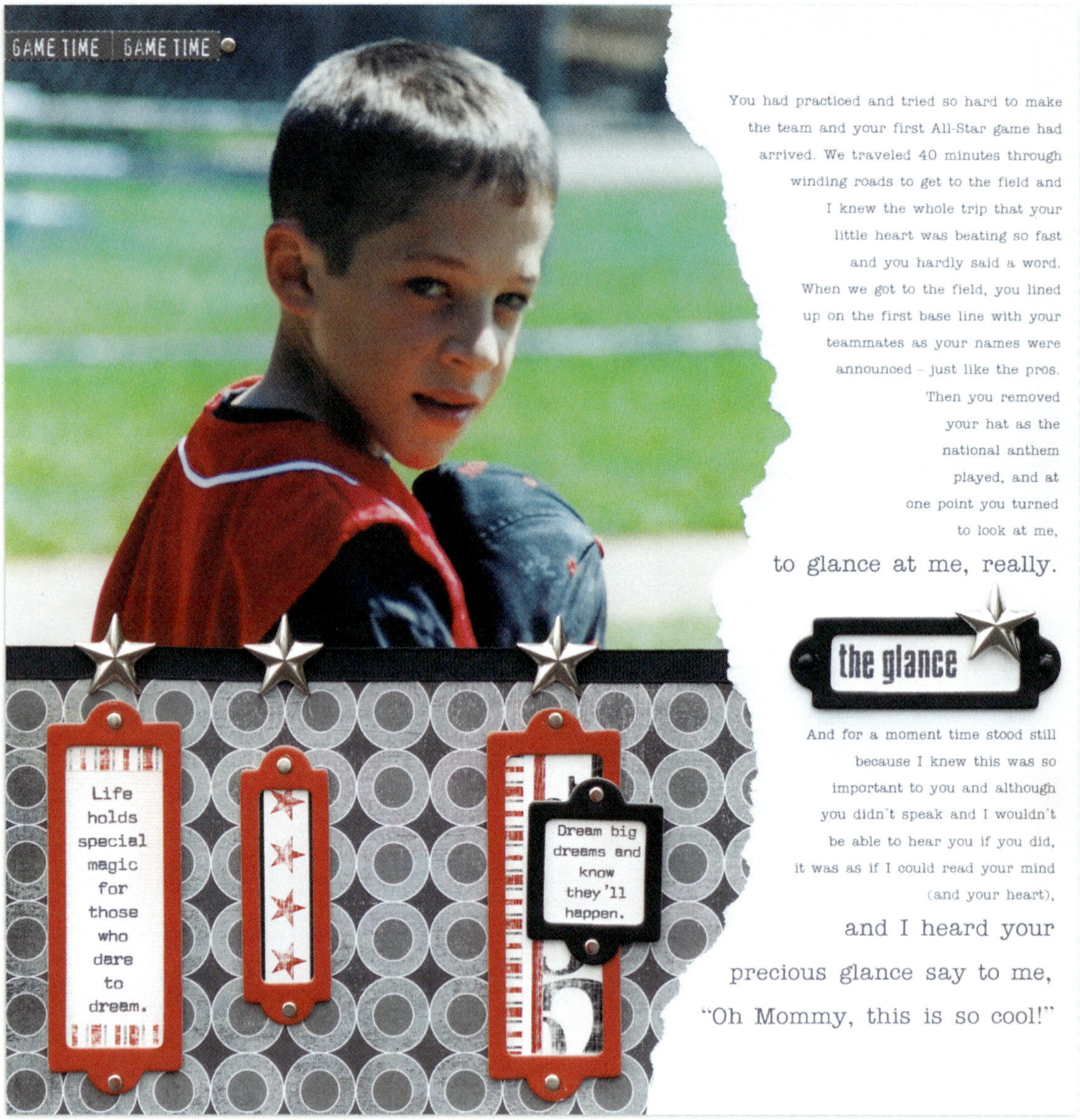

The journaling step in scrapbooking can be the most difficult one. Some of us sit down to journal and don't know where to begin. Others concentrate on the who, what and where of a layout, but wish they could include more personal thoughts. I've found that if I really listen to myself, the way I speak and think and get those thoughts on paper, I can translate them into a meaningful piece of journaling on my page.

Listening to yourself takes practice. Thoughts and memories are most likely replaying in your mind all the time; it just takes some practice to recognize them. When I notice myself thinking about a memory or aspect of life, I try to expand upon it a bit more and write down my thoughts.

I don't do this in an organized fashion. I grab a scrap piece of paper, a little notebook in my bag or a napkin and scribble down what I'm thinking. I write quickly so I can get everything down and don't pay attention to good grammar! I save my scrap pieces of memories and thoughts on a small bulletin board and then I can pull one down when I'm ready to scrap.

You may want to tape or staple your thoughts in a notebook or collect them in a file folder. It doesn't matter how it's done. The important thing is that you save your thoughts before they get lost and have them handy where you can easily get to them later.

How to Journal the Way You Think

1 Stop and Reflect
Stop and reflect once in a while during your daily routine or while looking at your photos. Try to listen to what you're really thinking.

2 Jot It Down
Jot it down! If you don't have a piece of paper nearby, use anything! Use the backs of receipts, restaurant napkins, kids' school papers - whatever you have at hand.

3 Save Everything
Save all your notes somewhere so they will be available next time you are looking for some thoughtful inspiration for your scrapbooking.

4 Avoid Distractions
When it comes time to journal these notes on a page, get rid of any distractions which may prevent you from writing the way you think. This may mean turning off the TV or music if words don't come easily to you.

5 Don't Stress About Grammar
Don't worry about grammar. Think of your journaling as a way to bring your thoughts to the page without rules. If it's one long run-on sentence, that's okay! What's important is it reflects how you think!

CAPTURING MOMENTS • 21

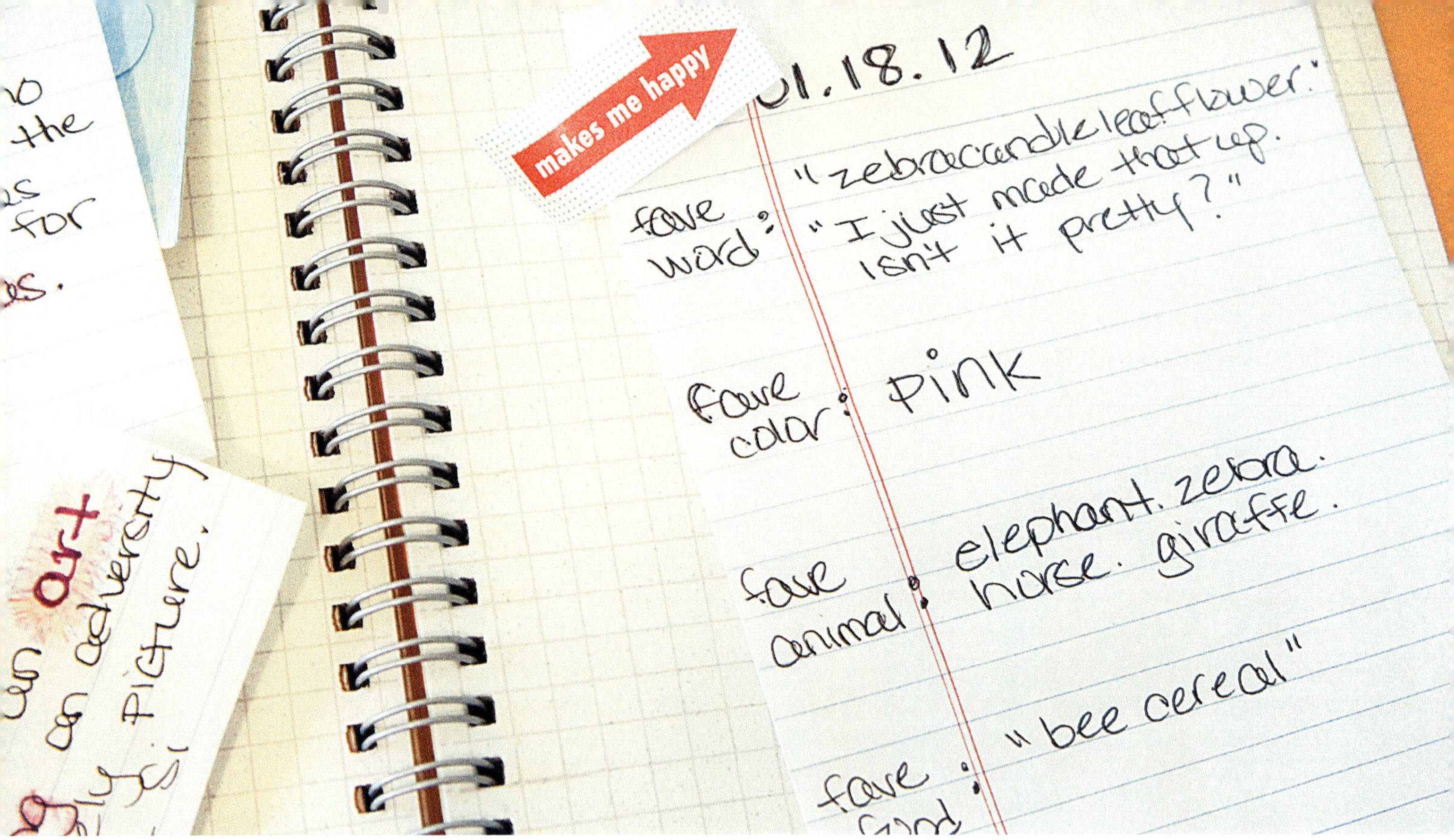

Documenting Everyday Dialogue
by Sara Gleason

Story lives in the things we say and hear: all the little conversations and dialogues with our loved ones, all the little things we say aloud to others and to ourselves, even all the little things we write in lists and letters and notes. The quirky speech *-isms*, the quotes and the chatter, all those spoken and written artifacts play like a soundtrack to our every day. Conversations and dialogues are some of the most authentic bits of ourselves and those we love.

Sometimes, these chatterings seem so ordinary to us that we run the risk of overlooking them in our memory keeping. Other times, something we hear or say strikes us so profoundly with its wisdom or humor that we are sure we will not forget it. But, if we don't take the time to actually put them on a page, this once memorable quotable fades away.

Several years ago I made a pledge to myself to document my personal soundtrack more intentionally. Most importantly, I try to record my family's dialogue right away. I often reach for whatever is nearby, but recently I've set aside a SMASH book solely for the purpose of curating our quotables. The book itself has become a treasured catalog of the things we say.

1 Document Family Quotables

Recently on President's Day, my daughter said, "Daddy could be president. But he doesn't have a president outfit. You really need a tie for that." Using my phone, I posted the quote word for word as a Facebook status message and retrieved it when I was ready to scrapbook.

2 Document Conversations

Take time to listen closely to the daily conversations that happen among family members, with friends or co-workers. Document exchanges that stand out, that reveal special bonds or make you laugh. They might be dialogues you participate in or those you overhear.

3 Create a Portrait

Capture the personalities of your loved ones by documenting the little verbal *-isms* they say. Not too long ago I painted a word portrait of my daughter by documenting her dialogues and inflections at that time. This kind of documentation paints a picture of the relationships and seasons in our lives.

4 Document a Q&A or Interview

Actively pursue the documentation of dialogue by conducting a Q&A and scrapbook the results. I used this approach when creating a page documenting my daughter's thankfulness as we sat down together at Thanksgiving.

5 Document Written Conversations

We tend to think of conversations happening verbally. Dialogues happen in other ways, too. Consider the back-and-forth of ongoing discussions that live in written words; these reveal a lot about relationships. From light-hearted text messages to more emotive letters, story exists in words shared but not spoken.

Prepare for Scrapbooking Using an iPad and the Apple iPhoto App

by Renee Pearson

I love my iPad. Not only does it allow me keep track of my business no matter where I am, it also helps me keep up with my Project Life scrapbooking. Since I don't have time to create scrapbook pages every day, I rely on my iPad as a way to keep track of my photos and memories. When I'm ready to sit down and scrapbook, I have everything I need stored right there on my iPad.

I use my iPhone camera exclusively since it's always with me. I learned how to take great photos with it from Molly and Jim Newman in their iPhone photography class, *iShot That!* My favorite photo-taking app is Camera+. It runs rings around the iPhone's Camera app and its built-in editing tools are fantastic. I no longer have to edit my photos in Photoshop before using them in layouts because they're ready to scrap right out of my camera.

At the end of each day, I transfer my photos to my iPad using the PhotoSync app. When I'm ready to start organizing, I turn to iPhoto for iPad and iPhone. It is a powerful app and it's worth spending some time getting comfortable with the many features. The help system is always accessible and easy to understand. The feature I use to organize for scrapbooking is called *Journal*.

With *Journal*, I select a group of photos and iPhoto automatically flows them into a journal that I can personalize. iPhoto adjusts the page around whatever you're doing. You can even add captions, maps, dates and weather giving yourself the big picture when you're ready to scrap.

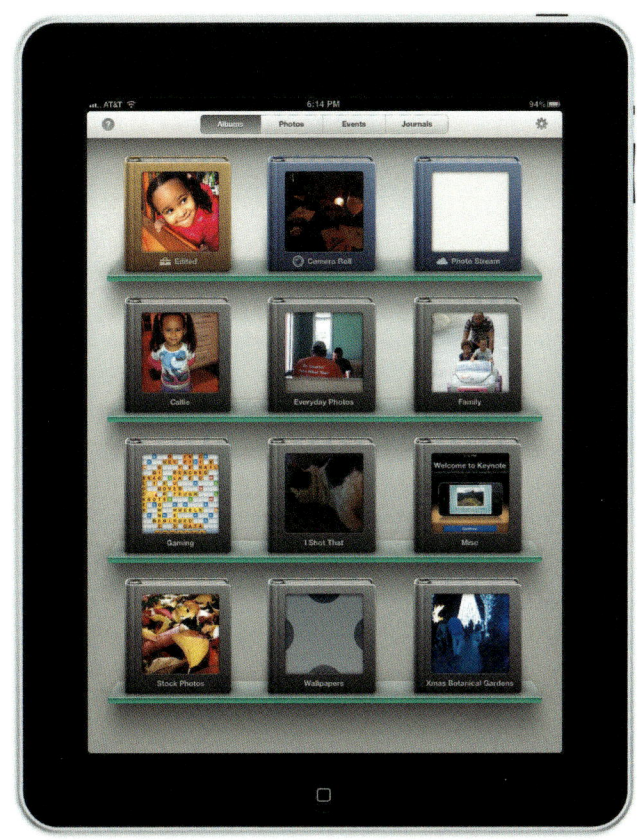

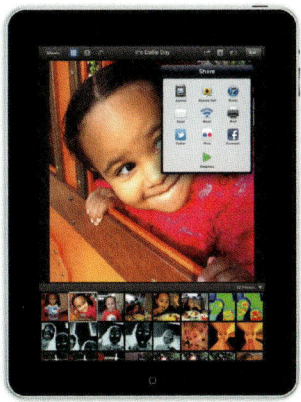 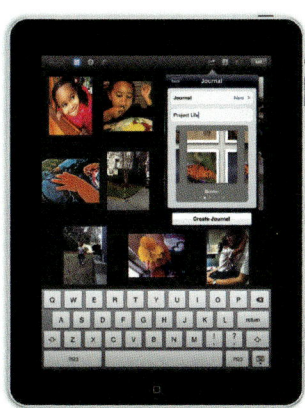

 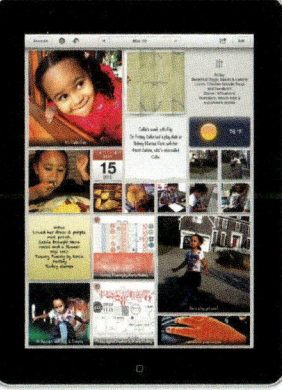

Tips for Customizing Your iPhoto Journal

- To resize a photo, tap to select it then drag one of the selection handles.
- To remove or edit a photo, tap *Remove* or *Edit* from the menu that appears directly above the photo.
- Move a photo by touching and holding it then drag it. Tap *Add a Caption* to type a caption inside a photo.

CAPTURING MOMENTS • 25

Telling Stories

Memory keeping invites us to explore the most precious parts of our hearts, revealing the truth behind our stories. This journey requires practice and the skill of being open and brave in our storytelling.

Looking Forward and Back to Create Meaningful Stories

by Kristin Rutten

I am no stranger to feeling stuck with my scrapbooking. You know, that place that can swing between feeling totally uninspired (as in *Who is really going to care about my boring life, anyway?*) to so overwhelmed with all of the details of life that are passing by undocumented that it seems futile to even try. Over time, however, I've learned that if I can just step back, remind myself why I'm scrapping in the first place and regain my focus as a storyteller, the floodgate of ideas opens up again, the guilty feelings are put to rest and I'm on my way to creating the kinds of pages I most value.

Why I Scrapbook

My primary goal as a memory keeper is to create an authentic representation of what it is like to be me as I go through life, as an individual as well as a mother, wife, daughter, sister, friend or any of the other roles I play. In a world that can often be very impersonal, I feel a need to share more of the real me, to be known and understood, particularly by those I care about. Scrapbooking is one of my avenues for doing this.

In a small way, I think of myself as a historian, but not the type who writes those dry high-school textbooks. Names, dates, locations... those details generally mean very little to me unless they help me understand more about the experiences of the people involved. I want to document the same kinds of things about my life that I personally find interesting about those who came before me: what it was like to live in a certain time period, how it felt to go through a particular experience, the reasoning behind the decisions that were made, the little details of daily life that probably seemed mundane at the time but that are often so very interesting in hindsight.

I want to capture the experiences of myself and my family, but my focus isn't so much on the who, what, when and where as on the *why*. It is this focus to which I return when I find myself getting stuck in my scrapping. To find this focus, I typically ask myself a series of questions.

A New Perspective

If I'm struggling to pinpoint the story I want to tell, I find it helpful to put myself in the shoes of those I envision looking at my layouts in the future.
- What will they find interesting about this story?
- What might have changed by that time that will make today's story more meaningful?
- What details can I share that seem obvious now but could easily slip from memory years down the road?

If I'm having a hard time imagining the future, I try to go into the past and imagine how the story might have been different if it had happened in another time period. If the experience had happened to my mother or grandmother, for instance, what kinds of things would I be interested in hearing about now? If I could go back and ask my ancestors how they felt about a similar experience, what would I ask them? The world changes so quickly and even seemingly simple things like how we feed our families or what we do on the weekends—even the cost of a gallon of milk or gasoline—may be very different than it was just ten, twenty or thirty years ago. Wouldn't it be interesting to be able to re-live a day in the life of your grandmother or great-grandmother through their scrapbooks?

Thinking about these things helps me identify the parts of my everyday life that I want to capture for later, for myself and those who come after me. It helps me find what is really interesting about my life, even when my life feels pretty routine and boring. It also helps keep the guilt monster at bay by relieving the urge to capture every single detail of every single day and instead focus on the bigger picture. And for those times when I'm so stuck that I can't even think of the questions, that's when I turn to outside sources such as the books we offer at Log Your Memory, the Internet or other sources of scrapbooking or journaling prompts.

Four Tips for Prioritizing Creativity Every Day

by Cheryl Ashcraft

Scrapbooking is not just a hobby for me; it's an integral part of my everyday life. It's not easy dividing time between daily chores and scrapbooking, but I've found a way to do both every day. Follow these four simple steps to make scrapbooking a daily occurrence in your life as well.

1 Balance work and play.

Just like most wives and mothers, I have household duties that cannot be ignored. However, managing these tasks in a timely manner leaves me with more time for scrapbooking. To do this, use your microwave or stovetop timer and set it for fifteen minutes. As quickly and efficiently as possible, begin working on your daily tasks. When the timer goes off, you are free for thirty minutes to scrapbook. Alternate the timer in fifteen minute/thirty minute segments. In a six-hour period, you will complete three hours of chores and three hours of scrapbooking without feeling like all you've done is work all day or feeling guilty because all you've done is scrapbook.

2 Limit the amount of television you watch.

For the shows you can't miss, make sure you record them to minimize the time you spend watching commercials. If you don't have a recording device, use commercial times to complete small scrapbooking tasks like picking a photo or choosing papers and elements for your layout. If scrapbooking is important to you, make it a priority. Determine that you will carve out time in your schedule for being creative!

3 Keep your camera near you.

For a long time, I kept my new digital SLR safely tucked in my camera bag, but I found I was not using it frequently enough. Store your camera (and charging cord and/or batteries) in a location that's safe, but accessible, so you can grab it and capture all kinds of moments—big and small. All those photos will inspire you to create more layouts!

4 Be organized, but don't over organize.

I love for things to be neat and tidy, but one of my faults is that I can spend so much time organizing my scrapbooking supplies that I have little time left to scrapbook. Find a system that works for you so that you can easily locate your scrapbooking supplies on your computer without devoting extensive amounts of time to organization.

By using these four simple steps to make creativity a daily priority, you'll find that scrapbooking can be more than just something you do. It will become something you are.

Tips for Easy Guilt-Free Scrapbooking

by Traci Reed

I don't know about you, but I have a lot on my plate!

As a work-at-home mom of three boys, it feels like I never, ever get time to go to the bathroom by myself, let alone scrapbook. So how do we make time for scrapbooking when we're always on the go and how do we maximize the time we *do* have?

Six Tips for Scrapbooking on a Time Budget

1 Get Organized

There are many ways to organize your scrapbook supplies and photos; find a method that works best for you and implement it. I am a digital scrapbooker. I choose to have a scrapbooking folder with sub-folders by theme and organize my photos by year with subfolders. This system works best for me and I don't waste a lot of time in organizing software. You'll spend dramatically less time looking for something to scrap with if you're organized and you'll have more time to enjoy scrapbooking.

2 Journal Ahead of Time

I can't always scrap right when I take a picture and sometimes, in just a few months, I've completely forgotten the story that behind it. I suggest getting an app like Evernote (free) to track the things you want to scrap. The cool thing about Evernote is you can access your notes on your phone, tablet or computers so you can always add to them when you have that genius thought while stuck in the carpool lane. Being a busy mom, I'm often out and about so this is a wonderful feature for me.

3 Keep It Simple

There is a *lot* of pressure out there in forums and galleries to make *every* layout a work of art with 1.5 billion embellishments on it, but I'm here to tell you that if you keep it simple (no matter how you like to scrap), you'll take the stress out of scrapbooking and enjoy it again!

- Use templates or sketches. They make life so much easier and that's what they're there for!
- Make pages for you, not galleries. The gallery life of a layout is a day or two of views, but they are going to last forever in your photo albums.
- Ask yourself three questions: *Does it tell the story? Does it look cohesive? Am I happy with it?* If you can answer yes, then you're done!

4 Designate Regular Mommy Time

Set aside a block of time that's good for you and your family and *scrap*. It could be Sunday afternoon, Monday night or Thursday at three p.m. Make yourself your favorite drink, go in the office, shut the door and put Daddy on kiddo watch. A happy mommy who's taking care of herself with a little me time makes for a happy family. You deserve it!

5 Turn off the Internet

The internet can be our biggest distraction. I often find myself opening my browser by habit and losing big chunks of time in netlandia. Did you know that the average person spends an hour a day just browsing the internet? I think scrappers spend even more time online. When you're scrapping, turn it off!

6 Let. It. Go.

I haven't been caught up in my albums since 2005 and I don't think I ever will get caught up again. Scrap what's inspiring you at the moment; don't feel like you have to scrap chronologically. When you try and scrap according to ridiculous expectations, you'll find that you lose your mojo. Just remember that you may not get all your memories catalogued and it doesn't matter, your kids will love your albums no matter what!

Enhance Your Memory Keeping with Social Media
by Amber Ries

Aside from the process of being creative and artsy,

the thing I love most about scrapbooking is the memory keeping. I love telling a story, and even more than telling, I love going back and reading these stories later after I've forgotten them. My brain is like Swiss cheese, full of holes where the memories fall out faster than I can make them. To compensate, I've learned how to keep track. Years ago, I kept a journal. I have a stack of cloth-bound books filled with my loopy teenage handwriting that I rarely go back and read. These journals have become a part of my past, but I continue keeping track of my stories and memories through my blog, my Facebook account, Instagram, Twitter and sometimes emails. In this fast-paced world things have changed.

How I Use Social Media

I use these platforms to aid in my scrapbooking for the following reasons:

- Because I want to keep an up-to-date record for photos I have taken and ease the process of journaling.
- Because I have a pretty photo with no story.
- Because I have a great story with no photos.
- Because I come across pictures to which I have forgotten the story.

At this point in time, I consciously write in my blog to keep track of memories as they happen because I know I will forget. At the same time, there are many things I want to remember such as funny one-liners or a momentary feeling that does not warrant a full blog post. This is where Facebook works for me. The Facebook platform is perfect for one-line memories and fleeting emotions whereas the blog is ideal for long, involved stories and events.

Facebook allows you to post short status updates on a regular or sporadic basis. With the introduction of the new Timeline feature, Facebook gave its users the opportunity to search past status updates. What is the importance of this feature? The fleeting thoughts you recorded never expecting to see again are now at your fingertips for memory-keeping. You can now search for status updates from a month ago or a few years back, certainly sparking many memories from your past.

I recently pulled out some photos to scrap, but once I finished the layout, I realized I had nothing to say about them. They were cute, sure, but the story behind them was uninteresting and I had already scrapped similar pictures from that day.

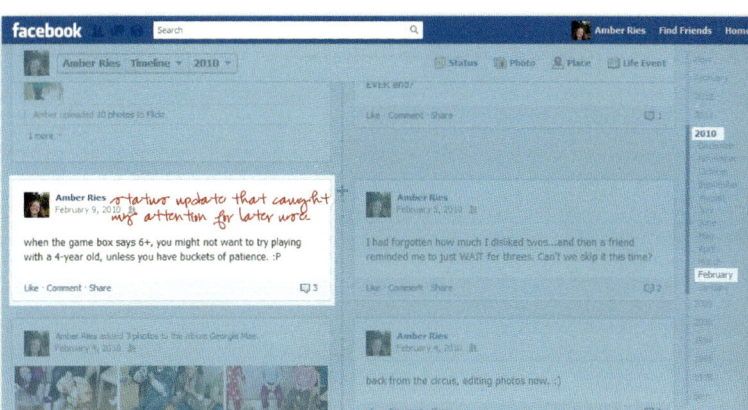

I found the answer to this problem by searching my Facebook status updates from that time period for inspiration. I found the perfect one I could use for my journaling and was able to finish the layout. You can use Facebook, Twitter, Instagram or other social media platforms in other ways as well:

- As stepping stones or idea triggers for layouts,
- To add interesting journaling for otherwise story-less photos, or
- As a jumping-off place for journaling.

When using the shorter status updates from these platforms it might be necessary to expand and elaborate; however, some status updates, curt and concise as they are written, might be just the words you need to tell your story and finish your layout.

Taking Stories from Blog to Page
by Christine Newman

One of my best secret weapons for scrapbooking is my blog, where I've been posting regularly for over five years. In 2009 I even blogged everyday for 365 days, sharing my daily photos and stories for Project 365. That was a huge undertaking that I haven't repeated since, but I do blog three to five times per week and tell my stories with photos and words. Blogging is something I've made a priority in my life. I find blogging the best way to get my stories down while they are fresh and it is where the bulk of my memories are kept.

Why I Blog

I don't scrap every story of my life, but when I do want to scrap a story, I often go to my blog to find the text/journaling from when it was fresh. Sometimes I copy and paste the journaling straight onto my scrapbook page. Other times, I add some additional journaling based on my perspective after some time has passed. In both of these instances, I'm incredibly grateful that I have the memories recorded on my blog so that I'm able to create pages with them.

One example of this is my digital page about going to a musical called *Mixtape* which I blogged about when it happened.

I copied and pasted the journaling from my blog post into this digital layout. And although I added and subtracted some text, the gist of that journaling came from my blog post.

I also use journaling from my blog for Project Life. I do a Month-in-Review blog post at the beginning of every month to summarize the prior month. This blog post contains a photo collage and some bullet points highlighting the month.

I save the photo collage in high-resolution so that I can print it out onto photo paper. I copy and paste the bullet points from the month into an 8.5x11-inch document in Photoshop and print it out onto white cardstock, leaving some room to adhere the photos. The result is a double-sided, 8.5x11-inch layout that I put into my Project Life album every month.

I love blogging as a form of memory keeping. I love even more that it is my go-to resource for scrapbook-page making. I record memories while they're still fresh and I can make a scrapbook page later based on my posts. There's no guilt of trying to keep up with memory keeping because the memories are already kept on my blog. They are there for the taking when scrapbooking inspiration hits!

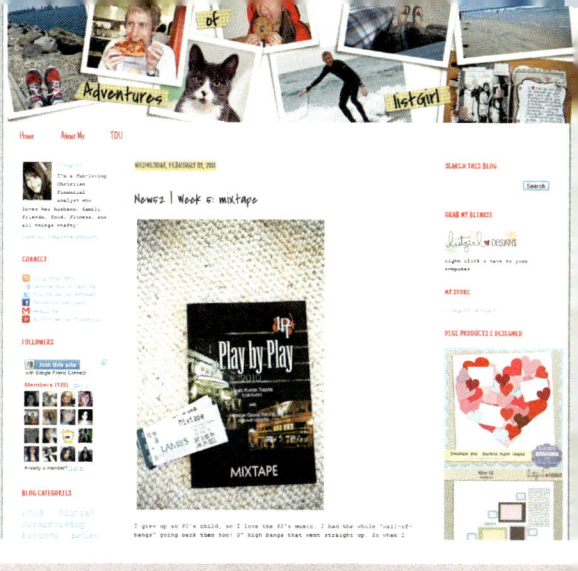

Fast and Easy Journaling with Lists

by Elle Price

Journaling is such an important part of my layout process but, I have to admit I struggle sometimes with finding the right words. Sometimes, when I'm scrapping a more generic photo, a photo that is similar to one I've scrapbooked before or I'm unsure of the story behind the photo, I hesitate when deciding what I want to capture and share in my journaling.

If I ever find myself struggling with the journaling portion of a layout, I have one go-to option that almost always works wonders: making a list! Making a list really takes the pressure off because you can use short sentences to get your points across. And, I think that when you don't feel as pressured to journal, the words come much easier.

For this layout, I used the title of my list for the title of my layout, too. It's a great way to tie them together and bring the focus in.

There are plenty of lists you could make from almost any photo and if you ever find yourself stumped on what to say, I encourage you start numbering or grab a numbered journaling tag and start putting a list together.

Kickstart Your Journaling

Here are just a few ideas for lists to use to kick-start your journaling:

- Things that make you smile
- Things I did today
- My favorite moments with you
- This year you did these incredible things
- Today's (this week's, this month's) top moments
- Things that make you giggle
- Your loves, right now
- Your favorite things to say (do, places to go, etc.)
- Things I want to do before I turn (insert age)
- My dreams (goals, etc.) for this year

TELLING STORIES • 39

Journaling from the Heart
by Heather Prins

> They melt me. Deep into my heart, their light shines, filling me with such sweet love. I'll never forget seeing them for the first time, two slanty pools, all watery and ink in color, just minutes old. My sweet baby boy, I fell instantly in love with you. Because of you, I am a mom. I catch my breath when I look into those beautiful eyes now, all blue with flecks of gold and green. Now, you are my oldest child, my only son, but still my baby boy. And those same eyes lead me straight to YOUR heart, whether it is through your laughter or through tears pooling, threatening to fall, I can see you. And I love you with all my heart.

Those Eyes

I am a writer. No, not in the professional-never-make-grammatical-errors kind of way, but a storyteller. I write from the heart, with my whole heart. Sometimes, my journaling is filled with emotion, written through tears streaming down my face and other times, I get caught laughing out loud as I am typing! But one thing is for sure, I love to journal on my pages. It was this need to tell my stories in their entirety that led me to digital scrapbooking in 2009. I instantly fell in love, not only with the numerous fonts available to me, but with the freedom to write anywhere on my layouts!

And so I write. I write with a sense of urgency of tomorrows that are not promised and kids that grow up way too fast. I write to try to stop time, if only for a few minutes, and to preserve a story for a lifetime. I write to leave not only a piece of my heart behind, but also my voice.

Words are powerful. Sometimes as a mom, my words are not always heard when they would be most effective, so writing to my children on my layouts allows me to communicate my feelings to them, especially when I am worried or concerned about them. Sometimes, for my loved ones, reading my words allows my voice to be heard.

The saying goes, "a picture is worth a thousand words," and while I believe that to be true, I also believe that having the stories to accompany those photos is a priceless treasure that transcends generations. If I handed a regular photo album to my kids, they might flip through a couple of pages and then it would be set aside, left untouched for I don't know how long. But handing them a book full of layouts with words on the pages, my words or their words or even words spoken about them by other people, entices them to keep reading and turning the pages. I see smiles flicker across their faces and a look of understanding when they have read one of letters I have written to them. Then, I know that I have done it; I have journaled from my heart.

> **Friday at last.** I had a great, relaxing morning. I played around in Photoshop and even managed to get a couple of layouts done uninterrupted. In the afternoon I helped Lexi work on another digital layout. I am so happy to be teaching her how to scrap digitally. But the fun ended when I got a call from the Citadel. Apparently my mom had been sitting by the front door since 9 a.m. this morning waiting to get picked up. It was now 1:30 p.m. That was not like her, so I quickly went up to check on her. When I arrived, there she was, waiting by the door and of course when she saw me her face lit up like a child's.
>
> I knelt down in front of her and gently asked her what she was doing. She said she was coming over to my place. I asked her how she was going to get there and she said she was going to call a taxi (she doesn't know how to call one, thank goodness). I asked her if she knew my address and she said no. I looked into her beautiful eyes and just waited. A few seconds later I saw that she was "back." She realized she didn't know what she was doing. I said, "Let's go upstairs and have a rest."
>
> I took her back to her room and she sat back in her big chair. She was normal again, I could tell. I left her for a while and came back later, by then she was joking about trying to escape the care centre. It made me sad, though, that she was gone from reality for such a long time. That's the first this has happened since her trauma nearly three years ago, but it is normal with the progression of dementia. The rest of the day I kept seeing her eyes in my mind, cloudy with uncertainty. I thought about how much I will miss seeing her eyes when she is gone from me. And so I worry that she will slip from me more and more and maybe one day, I won't be able to bring her back. Don't go Mom.

TELLING STORIES • 41

Use Little Memories to Celebrate Big Stories

by Jennifer S. Wilson

Every scrapbook page I create begins with a photo but that is rarely how it ends. I tend to use images as springboards for stories that are bigger and broader than what is captured by the photograph.

I am not a particularly prolific scrapbooker, mostly because my time is limited. That's why I work hard to make every page really matter. By thinking beyond the moment in my photo and letting my mind wander, I am able to document more of the stories I most want to remember.

There are four techniques I regularly use to dig deeper in my storytelling and find the one- thousand words of meaning behind my pictures.

1 Celebrate Relationships

Although a trip to California is the subject of the photos in this example, I journaled about my relationship with the person I went to see. I most wanted to remember how I valued our long friendship and how we have made time to see one another after moving far apart.

2 Celebrate Change

The photo in this example is simply of my daughter lying on the couch but the hidden journaling is about the surprises I was experiencing as she grew so quickly in front of me. I most wanted to remember what this rapid pace of change felt like and my expectations which were challenged in my role as a new mom.

3 Celebrate Traditions

This example is not about one particular Easter. In fact, I edited two photos from two different years similarly to tell the story of what happens year after year in our extended family. I most wanted to remember some of the specific details of how we make this holiday special for the kids.

4 Celebrate Journeys

The photos in this example document a road trip but my journaling honors our past, present and future. The most meaningful part of this story is what is not seen in the photos: my pregnancy. I most wanted to remember how this trip was symbolic of a new adventure for our family.

TELLING STORIES • 43

Inexpensive Details for Heartfelt Stories

by CD Muckosky

A canvas hangs by my desk as a reminder to Think Big. Thinking big often means recycling and re-inventing what I already have in front of me. I don't let high-priced products or the latest trends dictate how my tales must be told. I tap into my heart, add a little creativity and let the stories of my life unfold in front of me for little to no cost.

To make this process simple, I keep a recycle bucket close by for all the little bits of life that have nice colors, shapes or just might be useful later. When these items are sitting right beside me, I find they're more likely to become the bits that help me tell heartfelt stories.

In these three examples I will share a snapshot of my thought processes in creating heartful art. By incorporating recycled bits chosen with purpose into my artwork, I leave a little bit of me in every piece.

1 Think Big
TOTAL COST: $3

I started with a yogurt box top. The pink and green of this item was my color inspiration for the whole piece. I dug into my recycle bucket and discovered a rounded card from the packaging of a pair of tights. With a few stitches it became a lovely patterned piece. An old phone book page under colored vellum adds a subtle print to tie in with the print transferred on the background. Shavings from my favorite pencils were used to create an organic and simple flower. A small piece of leftover upholstery fabric, frayed and imperfect (like me), adds softness to the piece and reminds me that the best treasures might just be the imperfect pieces in my life.

2 All About the Tutu
TOTAL COST: $1.76

I like to have many layers on my pages. This can be done without feeling overcrowded or chaotic if you use a common color, shape or pattern to tie the layers together. For this page, it is circles. There are dots on the paper and circles created by stamping with found objects. I had a bottle top, bubble wrap and the head of the screw handy for this purpose. For the journaling I dropped alcohol ink onto the back of clear packaging to echo the circle theme. Scotch tape grounds the words (yet still is slightly transparent) and I used some tulle left from sewing a tutu to reinforce the subject while adding softness over the patterns.

3 What a Guy
TOTAL COST: $0

I have the most amazing husband. When I saw these pictures I knew this was the perfect place to tell the story of how much he means to us. The background is a cardboard box flap used as a blotting mat on my desk. I was careful on this page not to add too much that might distract from the photos or journaling. I laid out his boot lace to act as a frame and direct the eye through the pictures. I used stitching to frame the writing and make it the focal point. In the bottom corner I tucked in a box top with the number three circled (for *I love you*), leaving a secret message to him. I grounded this part with a piece of left over corkboard.

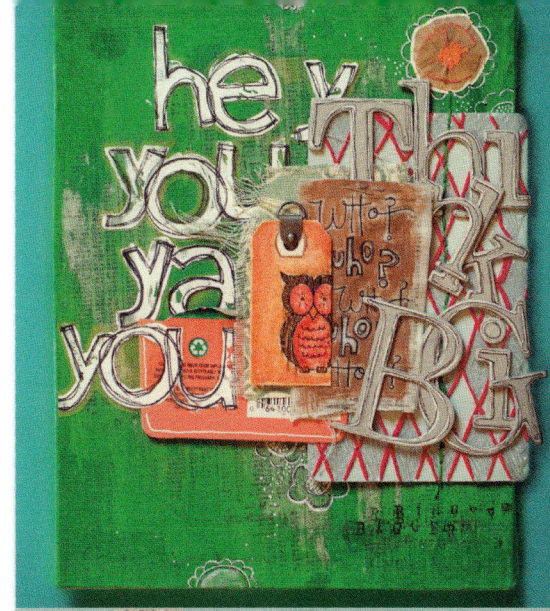

TELLING STORIES • 45

Creating Memories

Scrapbooking honors our most important memories with creativity. By embracing practical approaches for creative pages and projects, we allow the magic of storytelling to be shared with joy and ease.

almost 5

grow

Defining Your Scrapbooking Style Recipe

by Melissa Stinson

Most scrapbookers go through a period in their creative careers where they feel like they're in a rut. Not the *I-don't-feel-like-scrapping* kind of rut, but the *all-of-my-pages-look-the-same-to-me* kind of rut. It can be a scary place that leaves you wondering if you've spent all the creative energy you've been allotted in this lifetime. I went through a similar scenario not so long ago. My scrapbooking style had taken a massive overnight shift and for several months I happily chugged along, churning out layouts that I loved. Then, one day something just hit me and I started to wonder if I wasn't just making page after page of the same thing - if I wasn't as creative as I thought I'd been all along. If, perhaps, I was in a scrapbooking rut.

Luckily this rut occurred during the Christmas season when holiday recipes abound, especially those for Christmas cookies. Baked confections and memory keeping may seem like far-removed topics, but I came across a recipe for sugar cookies that literally changed my outlook on my creative process.

The basic premise is this: you start with a basic dough recipe which you make in a fairly large batch. The rest of the recipe proceeds to describe the many different cookies that can be made with just minor modifications to the prepared dough. By adding additional ingredients, forming the dough into different shapes or by adding a special type of edible decoration, the basic sugar cookie is transformed into something completely different from its original form.

I realized the same thing applied to my scrapbooking. When looking at my pages, I found that they didn't actually all look the same in the end, but they did all begin in the same fashion. After I finished the initial process of getting a layout started, I would always add little variations, making every page unique, just like that sugar cookie recipe!

You may not have recently undergone a massive style shift and in fact, you may have not even discovered your own personal scrapbooking style yet, but the exact same principle still applies to you. Your so-called scrapbooking rut most likely means that you've found your ideal way of scrapbooking, your sugar cookie recipe for pages. I can't pin-point your own personal sugar cookie style, but what I can do is show you my go-to process for making pages.

These four basic steps are how I begin almost every layout: they're my sugar-cookie recipe. They only take fifteen to twenty minutes to complete, leaving me plenty of time to work on any variations I want to include like additional layers and little embellishments.

To identify your own sugar-cookie scrapbooking recipe, start by looking through your layouts to identify common elements, themes or frameworks that appear on your pages. Make a list of those items and use that list to start the process of putting a page together.

My Scrapbooking Recipe

1 I start with a selection of products I think I want to scrap with and add in a base for my layout.

2 I add a photo (or photos) and, usually at this point, I also mat the focal-point photo with a bit of patterned paper.

3 I add strips of paper to the top and bottom (or perhaps the sides if I feel like making a variation) of the base page since I've found that this helps me define my layout's overall color palette.

4 I choose lettering that works with the color palette defined in my previous steps. I often temporarily form titles on plastic rulers instead of placing them directly on the page.

CREATING MEMORIES • 49

Designing Successful Page Layouts with a Sketchbook
by Tiffany Tillman

Before the masterpiece was etched into stone, a sketch was made. Before massive murals were erected, a sketch was made. Before man rocketed into the utter darkness of space, a sketch was made. Sketching is a timeless part of the design process, as old as the days are young.

Many scrapbookers tend to bypass this important step in the layout-creation process because sketching seems unnecessary. It's deemed a complete waste of precious creativity time, but that's the furthest thing from the truth! Old-fashioned sketching is extremely worthwhile for scrapbookers and is essential to my personal process. Here are five reasons why sketching works.

1 ## Sketching concentrates creativity on design.

Choices for colors, photos and words are unimportant while structure of design becomes the pure focus. Nothing speeds up overall page production like separating your design choices into bite-sized, manageable parts.

2 ## Consistent sketching builds efficiency.

Sketching allows you to generate multiple ideas relatively quickly. In one hour, I can draft five 3x3-inch thumbnails of layout designs. Completing five new ideas makes better use of my time by far than just building single-page layout.

3 ## Sketching helps manage details.

I add notes to my thumbnail drawings to specify areas of interest or concern. For example: *Masking Effect Here.* If the effect makes it into my final page, great! If not, how much time did I waste by including it in my sketchbook? Five seconds. I can live with that!

4 ## Sketching identifies recurring patterns.

Your signature style will jump out at you after a few pages of tiny drafts. You'll notice style changes or design ruts. And with that diary of creativity, you'll be empowered to step into new territory without committing to finished pages.

5 ## Sketching permits exploration.

And finally, sketching frees you to let loose and draw independently without criticism or critique. Mistakes, impossible designs and ideas that will never become scrapbook pages are completely permissible. Sketching gives you permission to explore the depths of your personal creative zones.

It's no wonder designers have sketched their way to new and amazing inventions. I make sketching the one of the first steps in my process because it works!

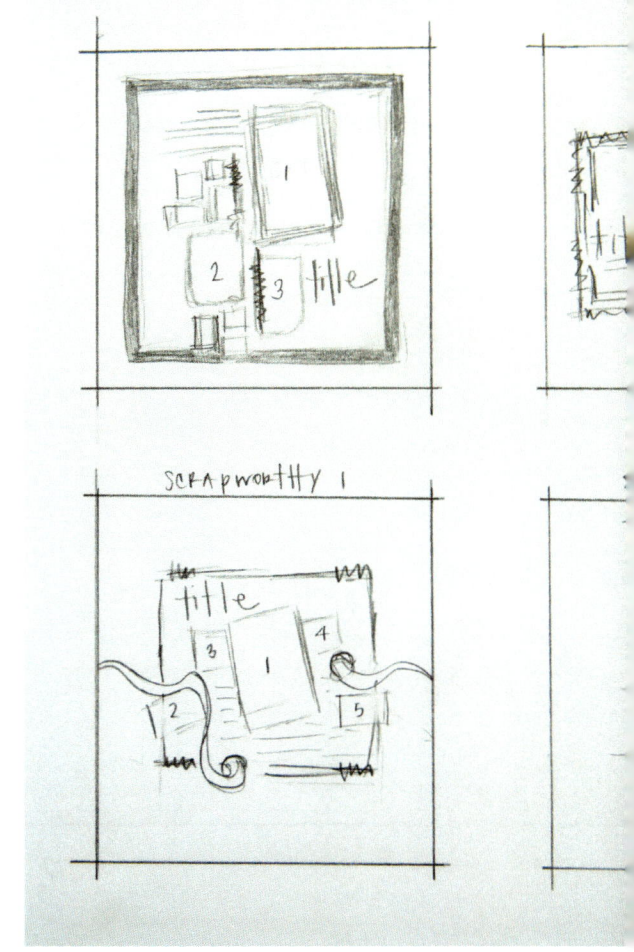

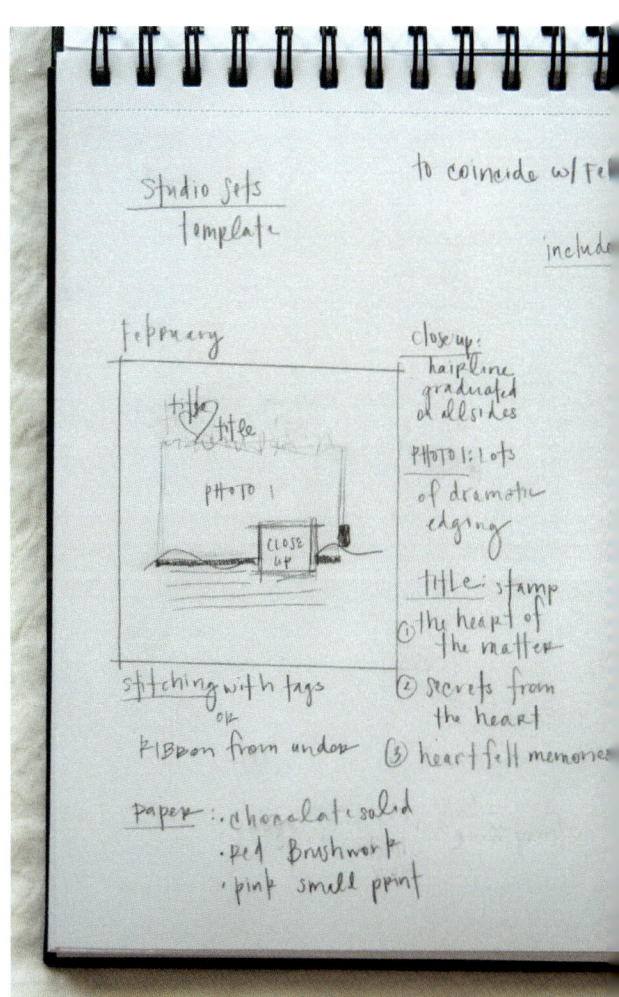

CREATING MEMORIES • 51

Improvisational Scrapbooking with Sketches
by Jenn Smith-Sloane

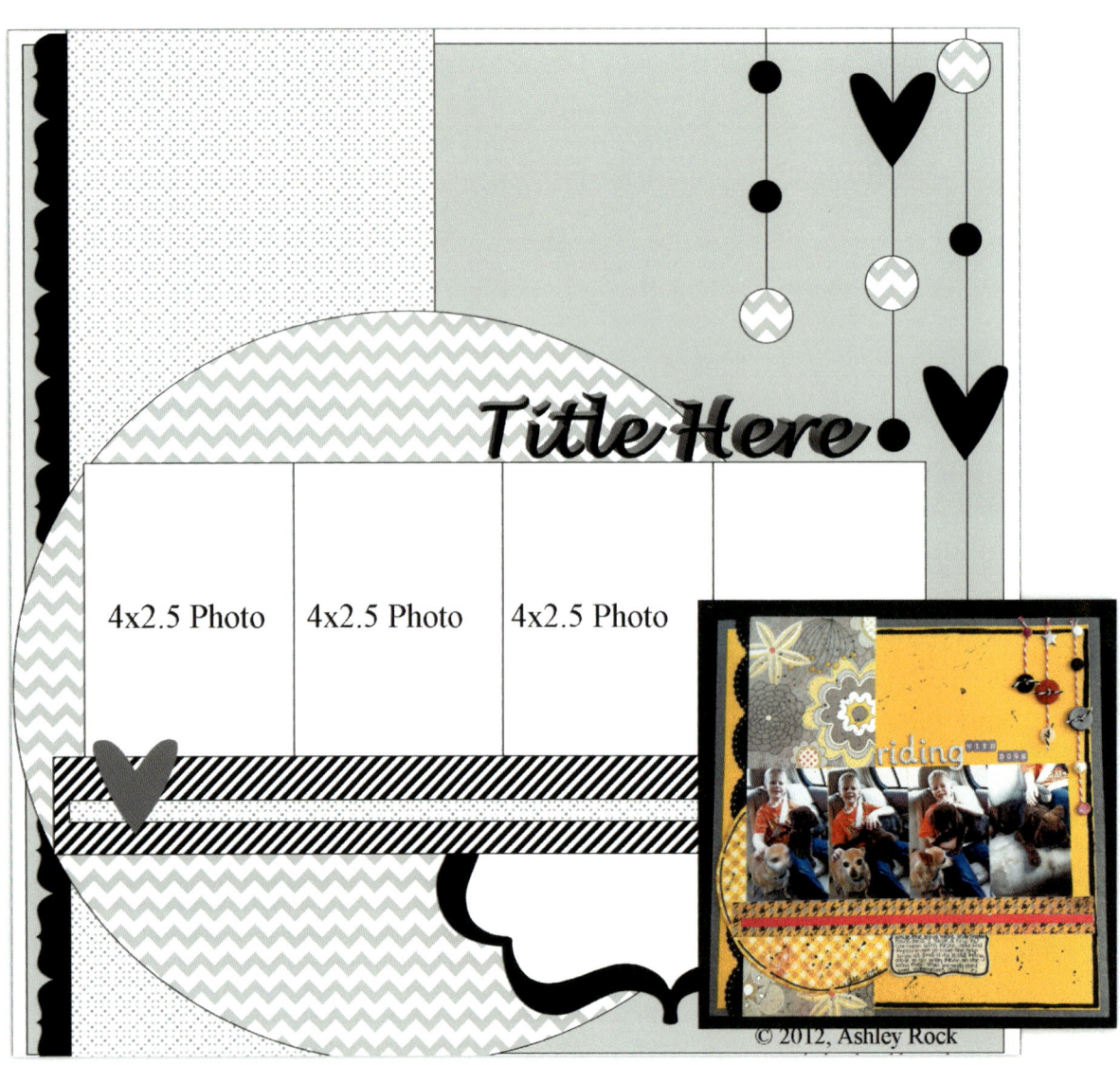

You have probably seen sketches on scrapbook

websites and blogs as well as in magazines. A sketch is a rough road map to inspiration for a scrapbook layout or card. The sketch artist gives suggestions for placement of various elements such as photos, paper, embellishments, titles and journaling.

What do you do, however, when there are parts of the sketch you don't like or you don't have in your stash? You do what I do: customize the sketch and make it your own. I like to think of the sketch as just a starting point for improvisation, not a finished design.

I start by choosing a sketch that works with the photos I have to scrapbook. Then I select a few basic supplies from my stash that I want to use on my layout. From there I let the sketch inspire me and then improvise on the details. In this example, I'll show you how I customized this sketch based on the tools I had and my own creative preferences.

1 The circle was a challenge for me as I have never owned a circle cutter. I grabbed a bowl from my cabinet and traced it with a pencil to make a circle. To hide the imperfections of my handmade circle, I inked the edges.

2 Adding texture or flat embellishments to background papers adds visual interest. My go-to approach is splatters of paint. I got my paint brush slightly wet and added some black paint. Then I held the end of the paint brush and tapped it randomly over the layout.

3 The sketch shows the title to be one long section in one font, I decided to change up the lettering styles.

4 I saw the stringed embellishments in the top right corner and knew I wanted to use twine. I cut three different lengths and adhered them down at the top to secure them before moving on.

5 I didn't want to use die-cut shapes because I wanted my focus to stay on the photos. I pulled buttons from my stash to match the colors in the layout. I also pulled out a few different brads and pearls.

6 I used ink and paint to finish the edges. To finish around the circle and journaling spot, I grabbed a thick marker. For the edges of the layout, I used paint and a thin paint brush.

CREATING MEMORIES • 53

Two Simple Shortcuts for Photo Arrangement
by Paula Gilarde

The biggest problem I have when scrapbooking is figuring out my photo placement. How many photos should I use? How should I configure them? The rest of the process is easier for me. I have a two key approaches to solving this problem:

1. Using digital frames, especially cluster or storyboard frames.
2. Using a sketch or digital template.

These two solutions provide some great design help when you are not sure how to arrange the photos on your pages.

1 Use a digital frame.

I use these for both my paper and digital layouts. Paper layouts come together very easily for me when I have my photo arrangement already done. Then, it's simply a matter of playing with papers and embellishments. Many digital designers have storyboard or photo-cluster products. The ones I use most frequently are by Katie Pertiet.

I typically start with my photos by selecting the ones I want to use and looking for an arrangement of frames that works with that number of photos. Next, I add my photos within the frames in my software, print and cut around the outside edge of the printed cluster. I used a digital cluster frame by Katie Pertiet that easily displays nine photos in my layout on the previous page about our trip to Storyland.

2 Use a sketch or digital template.

There are lots of sketch sites around the web and most digital stores sell digital templates which are the digital equivalent of sketches, only better. Did you know that you can use a digital template to make paper pages? You can use them to help you arrange photos. I used the *Caught on Film* layered template from Katie Pertiet as the basis for my Thanksgiving layout. I used the digital frame and the journaling spot from the template. Then, I used the template as a sketch for the rest of my design for patterned-paper and embellishment placement.

This is pretty easy to do. First, open the template in Photoshop or Photoshop Elements. Locate the layers for the elements you wish to use. Create a new canvas for the elements you want to print. In this case, you could print the entire frame cluster on an 8.5x11-inch sheet. Using clipping masks, clip your photos onto the photo placeholders by positioning the photos in the layer above and hitting *Shift-Ctrl-G* in Photoshop or *Ctrl-G* in Photoshop Elements. Create a new canvas to hold the journaling tag unless you want to print it on photo-paper. I created mine at 4x6-inches in size. Drag the journaling tag and text box onto the canvas. Add your journaling and print. I printed mine on patterned paper.

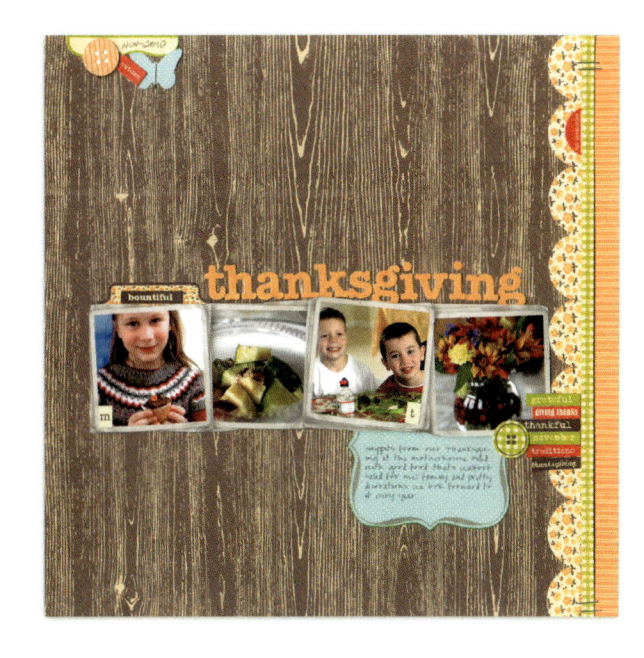

Create a Simple Vintage Collage In Three Steps

by Nancy Nally

At heart, I'm a clean and simple scrapbooker.

But, a part of me admires and covets the ability to recreate the messy randomness of the collage look even though it does not come naturally. After grappling with this problem over some time, I've found a solution that works for me!

I have evolved a three-step recipe which lets me quickly and easily create my own simple version of the vintage-collage look within the limits of my clean-design preferences.

Collage purists may say it's oversimplified, but it's a reliable shortcut that gives me results that I am happy with time after time. Plus, it works on everything from layouts to cards and tags.

This three-step recipe has become such a staple of my paper crafting that I now use it for almost every project. I have even started sorting my supplies and storing them by each step in the system. The recipe has become an efficient system for my creativity.

1 The Texture Layer

The first step that I take is to make sure there is some subtle texture in the background. This can be done in many ways. Sometimes a patterned paper will have visual texture to it or I can create texture with a stamp, distressing or embossing. Rub-ons also work. Use anything that is flat to the texture of the paper background but adds visual interest. I typically prefer light ink colors or paints if I'm using those mediums as the intent is to create interest without being distracting.

2 The Flat Layer

This layer could also be called the paper layer. While any effect created in step one is part of the background, step two is laid on top of the background and is very thin and creates a bit of depth. Typically, this layer is created from paper items such as patterned paper, cardstock stickers, punches or die cuts from cardstock-weight material. I leave quite a bit of white space because I find it is easier to add more later than it is to have no room to add the item you want.

3 The Dimensional Layer

This step is where my project finally starts to look more collage-inspired because I add the real depth that distinguishes the collage look. This dimension can come in the form of any 3D embellishment, preferably multiple ones. I use brads, flowers, chipboard, buttons and rhinestones regularly - anything that has bulk to it will do.

I implemented the three-step simple collage on the layout on the previous page about my daughter's recent trip to see her first movie in a theatre. I started by stamping the background with a Hero Arts Newspaper Background stamp. Then, I added paper layers consisting of the patterned paper strips, the stamped ticket strip and the journaling block. Finally, for my dimensional layer, I used a chipboard alphabet for the title and dimensional flowers.

CREATING MEMORIES • 57

Combine Your Go-To Foundations for Quick, Richly Layered Pages
by Debbie Hodge

There are several configurations of combined elements (photos, journaling, embellishments and title) I like to use again and again when making scrapbook pages. I use these configurations, or foundations, because they consistently yield well-designed pages. I reuse and combine these four go-to page foundations to quickly make richly layered pages. The resulting layouts are busier and more complex, but they come together quickly. Re-using and combining these favorite approaches is a great way to make layered pages that look different every time.

1 Band on Cluster

The key elements are all on the vertical band. By bringing in backup layering, the page gets the energy it needs. I re-used a cluster from a different page by opening the digital file and dragging all of the elements to this layout. I even kept two of the same patterned papers and the digital frame on this new design.

2 Block on Band

I began this page with a patterned-paper base. I used a blocked grouping to incorporate four photos, ephemera that supports my pawn-shop photos and a title. However, this overwhelmed an already-busy design. Trimming the patterned paper down to a band let me include it and ground the blocked grouping to the canvas.

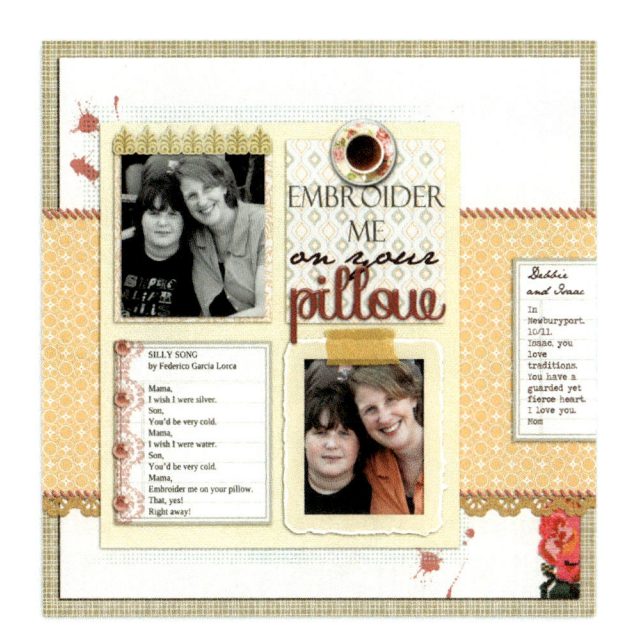

3 Grid on Block

Grid designs usually feel too clean and often don't provide enough space for using all of the papers and elements I enjoy adding. I re-used a similar configuration of blocks from another layout, but flipped them horizontally. Tone-on-tone patterned papers in blue and white keep the block in the background.

4 Grid on Band

I re-used a four-block grid arrangement from another layout, but changed the orientation from landscape to portrait. The blocks are on a cream mat and layered over a horizontal band. The band provides a home for the journaling that didn't fit in the grid. The band also lends itself to edging details that add interest to the page.

Simple Techniques for Visual Complexity
by Anna Aspnes

Complex and involved scrapbook pages can be quick and easy to create. Really! You can effectively trade difficult and time-consuming tasks for more simple techniques and still obtain similar results. It is not a matter of the type of techniques you decide to use in your pages, but more so the way in which you combine or stack them that counts. This simple layout incorporates a single photo, one-word title and story with just four additional elements. The layout looks as though it uses many more elements than this because of the complexity of the supplies I have chosen. Complex supplies typically have multiple colors or patterns and may include products such as intricate rub-ons or stamps, detail-oriented transparencies and overlays, colorful elements or artsy papers.

1 Supplies

The number and type of scrapbooking supplies you select for any given layout can have great impact on the complexity of the resulting page. Surprisingly, less is often more. Choosing fewer supplies with complex designs often leads the way to layouts that appear to have employed more difficult techniques and give the impression they have taken more time to put together.

2 Duplicate

You can use any element more than once to fill the canvas of your page and add detail. Duplicate the photo, title and/or any of your embellishments one or more times to create a more interesting layout. I duplicated the photo, title, mini brad, painted heart stamp and flower twice to create a trio of each element. Note that odd numbers of elements in a design are more pleasing to the eye than even numbers.

3 Resize

Adjust the scale of the elements on your pages to create visual variation. If you are a paper scrapbooker, you can use different sizes of a similar embellishment. Digital scrapbookers can resize the same element by selecting the *Move* tool from the *Tools* palette/box and dragging the bounding box inward or outward to decrease or increase the size of an element as desired.

4 Recolor

Vary the color of the same group of elements to further diversity the relationship between each component in the group. Change the color of one or more of your photos to black and white or sepia in tone or adjust the color of your elements using the *Hue* and *Saturation* tool in Photoshop to coordinate with the colors on your page.

5 Move

Rotate and/or adjust layers or elements to complete your page. Rotating adds interest to a group of elements and can transform a very linear layout into a more free-form and artsy creation. Moving elements around your page in a play-driven manner provides the opportunity for finding the best fit for each component.

CREATING MEMORIES • 61

Create Cohesive Layouts with Repetition

by Cindy Liebel

Repetition is a useful tool to use in designing scrapbook layouts. The story behind my *Seems Like Yesterday* layout is about how fast my daughter is growing before my eyes. How I cherish every waking moment of her existence and embrace all the fun things that come in little packages: hugs, kisses, cuddle time, etc. These are moments that I want to last forever. To make this page special, I repeated many details including textures, colors and shapes inspired by my photo.

I often repeat same type of elements continually throughout a page design. To accomplish this, I use a variety of tools such as punches and die-cutting machines to create my own embellishments. It's a fun way to tell the story and at the same time create good design flow.

Inspiration is found within the photos I use to scrapbook. In this case, the butterfly-printed shirt my daughter wears, the bright, pretty colors surrounded by neutral elements of the outdoors and the texture of the wood-grain bench she sits on inspired my overall page design. Bits of texture from the photos are carried throughout the layout and elements as well.

Before creating a page, I sketch several different design ideas and think about what tools I will use to create the elements on my page. Once I created a sketch for my page, I began by cutting out a variety of butterflies using a die-cutting machine and punches in all sorts of shapes and sizes. The texture from the wood-grain bench prompted me to use a wood-grain embossing folder on some of the butterflies.

I loved the effect it created and decided to do the same with a kraft envelope holder that will hold the hidden journaling. I punched a smaller butterfly out of a larger butterfly, which is a great way to use negative space within a positive element that is the same shape. Since there were a lot of different types of textured butterflies, I used a polka-dot embossed cardstock background.

Next, I printed out my photos in the size I wanted to use and began the building of my page design. I arranged photos and butterfly elements and determined what patterned paper to use and where the title and journaling will be placed before committing to a final design. A touch of machine stitching on the pattern paper and the textured kraft envelope added bits of extra texture to the opposite side of the page for balance. Lastly, touches of ready-made embellishments were added to give the butterflies a tad of color.

Other Ways to Incorporate Repetition

- Use photos that are printed and cut into a specific shape such as circles, flowers, rain drops, hexagons, etc. This is a great way to add a lot of photos onto a page. Plus, they act as more than just the focal point, but also as fun embellishments.
- Use shapes to create an embossed background for a tone-on-tone effect.
- Create a large element using the same type of shape in a smaller form. For example, create a large heart using punched hearts in smaller sizes arranged in a heart shape.
- Use repeated elements that do not necessarily go with the topic or theme of your layout. It's always good to play and experiment.

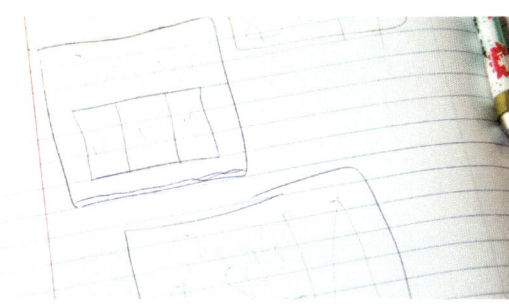

CREATING MEMORIES • 63

Using Digital Papers and Elements on Traditional Layouts
by Robyn Meierotto

When it comes to scrapbooking, it's either paper or digital, right? Well, I beg to differ. I like to shake things up and use digital papers and elements on my traditional paper pages. It can be quite addicting! Most paper scrappers rarely dig into online digital-scrapbooking stores, but they're a great thing, especially for those who don't have a traditional scrapbook store available.

There are an amazing amount of talented designers in the digital world. The kits are full of goodness at a great price and are infinitely reusable. Many designers of digital products also cross over into designing paper products, so the look you love might have extra designs available digitally.

I've done several hybrid pages and projects using printed digital supplies on my paper pages and I honestly can't tell the difference between regular paper supplies and digital papers and elements on a page.

To get started, I like to put a lot of different digital elements on one canvas in Photoshop to save paper and ink. I usually fill a letter-sized sheet and then print. I trim my papers, cut out my elements and even add in some other elements, papers and tools from my traditional supplies. After printing, it's exactly the same process as using traditional products.

In the layout on the previous page, all the papers (other than the background yardstick) are digital papers as well as the *Hello card* and the *happy happy* banner elements. The confetti is punched from digital paper as well. After putting all the parts of my layout together, I added stamping for the title, stickers, writing and finally stitching with my sewing machine.

In the layout on this page, all the papers except for the cardstock are digital designs and all the paper elements are also digital. I first printed on the cardstock background sheet before I started. The number spray and the number line are all printed right on the sheet. The only non-digital items are the washi tape, stitching and *happy* ticket.

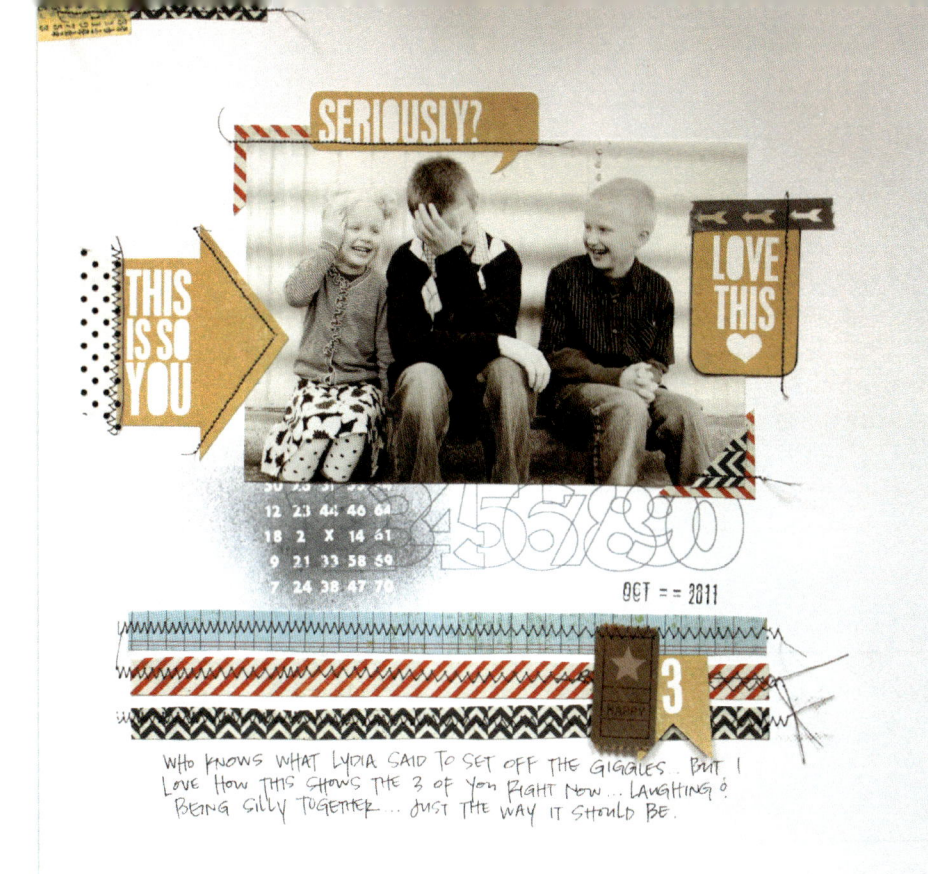

Get Started with Hybrid

You only need a few supplies for hybrid scrapbooking:

- A photo-editing program such as Adobe Photoshop or Photoshop Elements.
- A good printer. Photo printers are perfect for this as they deliver high-quality prints.
- A heavy matte-finish, high-quality paper.
- A few digital scrapbooking kits and downloads.

Easy Scrapbook Lettering with Alphabet Stamps
by Michelle Hernandez

I am a scrapper who hates her own handwriting.

No matter how much I try, the handwriting on my layouts never looks intentional. In fact, the more I concentrate on penmanship, the worst my spelling gets. So, I started using letter stickers, which gets really involved and painstaking. Stickers also take up a lot of storage space. My solution? Peg-mounted alphabet stamps. I find alphabet-peg stamps faster to use and easier to clean up than stickers. Plus, they take up less space.

Five Tips for Scrapbooking with Alphabet Stamps

1 Don't throw away the original box.

I used to put my stamps back after each single use but that got really time consuming. Now, I simply line them up in alphabetical order next to my project and put them back in the box right after I finish. I also altered the original box by cutting the top into a flap for easier access. A piece of tape prevents the stamps from flying everywhere when they get knocked over.

2 Vary the fonts of the stamps you use.

My favorites right now are Retro Typewriter and Swanky Uppercase ABC, a reverse-impression stamp. If you want a fun, ransom note-inspired look to your letters, press down firmly so the stamp edges also touch the paper. If you don't like messy, make sure to press lightly but for a little longer to leave a good, even impression.

3 Set up your words in advance.

This reduces spelling errors and speeds up the process.

4 When you make a mistake, cover it with a scrap and re-stamp.

This is what I had to do on my layout because I ran out of stamping space. I first hand wrote the middle of the quote, but that looked unintentionally messy, so I used letter stickers to save space. Make sure you don't run out of space by stamping a trial run on a paper scrap to see how everything fits. I tend to be impatient so I write the quote out first and stamp the words in reverse.

5 Neatniks might want to consider alternative stamps.

If you prefer perfectly aligned words, perhaps this isn't the optimal stamp method as you are stamping blind with wood pegs. Instead, use a ruled acrylic block and clear alphabet stamps so you can see where you are stamping.

CREATING MEMORIES • 67

Three Creative Ways to Use Stencils on Your Scrapbook Pages

by Amy Kingsford

Do you remember back when stencils were king? As someone who started scrapbooking in the late 90's, I am certainly no stranger to stencils. In fact, these nifty tools were right up there with decorative scissors and stickers on my list of go-to supplies. Oh, how things have changed in the past decade and a half! Now we have die-cutting machines, punches and alphas in every color and the idea of the stencil has become almost retro. What does this mean for those of us hiding a sizeable collection of stencils at the back of our stash? If you ask me, it means that it's time to bring the stencil back!

Below are three ideas to help you dust off your old stencils and start using them on your scrapbook pages again:

1. Use stencils to create a fun peek-a-boo effect with bold patterned papers.

In my page, *Here Comes the Sun*, I've layered some standard poster stencils over top of patterned fabric swatches to create a fun peek-a-boo effect in my over-sized title. You could also use this technique to create a fun alpha-grid foundation for your page or even to turn a single alpha into a focal element on your page.

Tip: For added dimension, use foam squares between your stencils and your favorite patterned papers.

2. Use stencils to add hand-stitched details on layouts and elements.

To make a simple but eye-catching hand-stitched tag, I converted an old vinyl stencil into what turned out to be the perfect stitching template. I simply used the inside edge of my stencil for punching my stitching guides into my tag using an awl. Then, I was able to go back through and stitch the design with embroidery floss and needle.

You can also use this technique to add hand-stitched details directly to your pages, including hand-stitched titles, hand-stitched frames or even hand-stitched borders!

Tip: Try placing your project and stencil over top of a cork tile or felt mat to make punching your holes quick and easy.

3. Use stencils to add glitzy details to your page background.

Here I've used a stencil to create some subtle glittery clouds on my page, *Tree Hugger*. I started by painting over a vinyl cloud stencil with a clear gel medium. Then, I quickly removed the stencil and sprinkled the treated area with glitter. Once dry, I chose to add a doodled border around the edge of my clouds to help them to stand out a bit more and add to the whimsical feel of my page.

Tip: You could also go for a clear-embossed or water-marked look with this technique by simply skipping the glitter and letting the clear gel medium dry on your page's background.

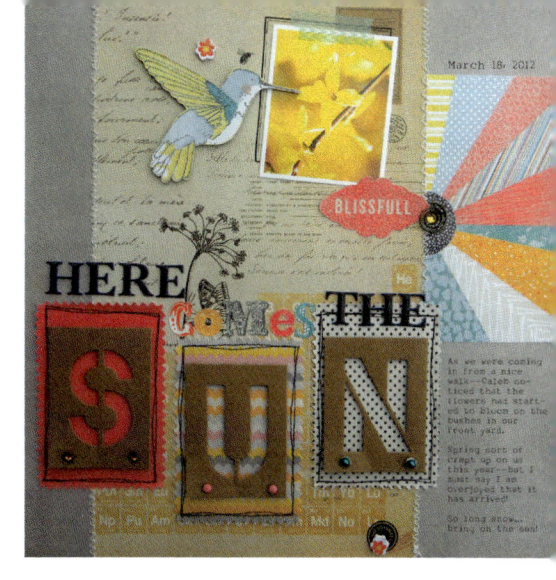

CREATING MEMORIES • 69

Wet Media: Three Easy Techniques for Layouts
by Ashli Oliver

For me, the excitement of scrapbooking is just as much about getting down and dirty as it is about having a beautiful, finished page. The sometimes unpredictable and free look of materials like wet media that move on their own lends a certain life to the page, but the only way they can get to your project is through the use of your own hands. I love how this can bring out the artist in any scrapbooker.

1 Watercolor Pencils

In the example at right, I played with watercolor pencils to create a simple polka-dot pattern that moves the eye across the page. After drawing rough circles using a waterproof pen, I scribbled with watercolor pencils. For easier blending, keep darker colors to the edges and lighter colors to the center. To avoid paper warping, I like to use watercolor paper. After blending with a small, wet brush, I let the circles dry. Then, I roughly cut circles of patterned paper for an accent on a few of the dots. Using patterned paper with a handmade pattern can help integrate the two.

2 Stamping with Paint

In the layout on the previous page, a simple shape constructed from cardboard scraps makes a great tool for stamping with paint. Any acrylic-based paint will work; I used leftover house paint. I first cut cardboard strips (roughly 2x4-inches) and then folded them into points. I used a stapler to join the pieces together, forming a star. Spread your chosen paint onto your craft mat. Coat the edges of your shape and then stamp.

3 Creating Translucent Paper

In this second example on this page, I took a beautiful patterned paper and made it translucent. You will need matte medium (find it in the art supply section of any craft store), a sheet or scrap of patterned paper and an old paint brush. Spread an even coat of the matte medium over the top of your patterned paper. Let dry then repeat. After the paper has two dry coats, soak it in a pan of cool water for one hour (or up to ten hours). Gently rub away the backing with the pads of your fingers. It helps to do this under running water, being careful that you do not tear the paper. After this is dry, you may notice a milky white look from residual paper fibers. Re-wet and rub this off. Once completely dry, you will be left with a semi-translucent piece of patterned paper.

Combining Wet Techniques

Now that we have seen three different techniques for using wet media on your layouts, I have put all of them (plus a bonus technique) to work on one layout. In the third example on this page, here's what I did:

- I stamped hearts with paint on the background.
- I drew hearts with my watercolor pencils.
- I cut hearts from translucent paper I created.
- I splattered ink across the page.

CREATING MEMORIES • 71

Documenting Real Life with Souvenirs and Ephemera

by Amy Tan

For as long as I can remember, I have loved collecting souvenirs. From travels near and far, I have cut out magazine clippings and saved ticket stubs to later be put in a safe place. That safe place, however, usually a box or an envelope that couldn't be easily preserved or shared, only served as a temporary place. Now that my love of scrapbooking has evolved, I am excited to have a system for all these little tangible bits of life. Incorporating actual memorabilia and souvenirs into my scrapbook albums and paper projects is something I love doing. Mini books and visual journals are my favorite way to showcase these types of keepsakes.

By preserving our real mementos and details of our lives, we're enhancing not only our memory keeping, but the experience as well.

Before many of my overseas travels (and domestic plane trips), I pre-make the cover and inside pages of a book that I take along with me. In addition, I pack a little kit containing basic supplies to help make the memory-keeping process an easy one. Documenting while on the go has enabled me to record memories that I may have forgotten if I waited until getting back home.

I always try and keep a tape runner in my purse. It comes in handy when we enter a restaurant and I can grab a business card and adhere it immediately on a page. After all, putting the card in right away can trigger the journaling for later. It also serves as a place holder for the event. It's nice to have not only a head start, but also a secure place for the memorabilia.

Business cards from hotels work nicely as well. Museums sometimes have business cards that can be included in your projects. Also, subway cards and tickets can make fun and colorful souvenirs in books. There are several additional techniques I use to create these on-the-go books.

Ephemera Tips

1 Keep It Simple
Adhere fabric paper to the cover of a Daybook, embellishing it simply. Then just add tickets and postcards while on the trip.

2 Embrace Randomness
Throwing in random objects, like the wrapper to a delicious cookie the hotel left when they did turn-down service, helps capture travel memories.

3 Include Found Paper
Incorporate brochures and maps, like a Paris metro map. It's nice to be able to preserve the quality of a fold-out element.

4 Use Washi Tape
Add a strip of washi tape on a double-sided item to create a flip-up element. This way the back doesn't have to be hidden.

Four Techniques for Building a Cohesive Mini Book

by Elise Cripe

Some of my favorite paper-crafting projects are mini books. I love how they can document a full event, adventure or season. I love that they can be completely different and that each one represents an opportunity to try a new style. When scrapping a mini book, I like to create continuity by designing each page so it works together with the whole project. I often unify each book by picking a color scheme from the start, but I also like to bring the content and story together through embellishment repetition. This can be achieved in many different ways but here I'll highlight four of my favorite go-to methods for creating cohesive mini books.

1 Shape repetition

When creating a 4x6-inch mini album to share photos of a trip to Palm Springs, I used circles over and over to tie the book together. They can be seen in the patterned-paper choices, font, stitched spirals and in the circle embellishments I freehand cut from coordinating patterned paper. You can easily achieve cohesiveness by using shapes, even if they are different sizes and colors.

2 Border repetition

In the small mini book I created about my trip to New York City, I used my sewing machine to add stitches in teal thread around the border of each page. The patterned papers and colors on each page vary, but they are each unified and pulled together because they have the same border.

3 Technique repetition

I love to add clear transparencies (sold at office supply stores) to my albums because they create floating embellishments. For my honeymoon mini book, I combined transparencies with ruffled fabric to act as a simple embellishment in my photo-heavy 4x6-inch book. I cut strips of fabric, sewed them to clear pages with my sewing machine and added an embellished page between every few photos. Any technique could be used but I love ruffled fabric for the extra texture it gives my albums.

4 Journaling repetition

I like to create small albums while I am traveling, but I don't like to carry a lot of tools and products with me. In 2008, I took a trip to Hawaii and committed to using only found papers and Polaroid photos to create the whole album. To unify all the stuff I was collecting, I used simple manila tags from an office supply store. Each tag represented a day of the trip and I stamped it with the date. On the back, I wrote in list form everything we did that day and then let the papers and few photos speak for themselves. This book is a true collection of mixed paper, but is all tied together through the repeating tags.

CREATING MEMORIES • 75

Tracking Your Scrapbook Supplies with Spreadsheets
by Lauren Reid

Keeping track of your scrapbooking supply list isn't something that pops into your mind too often during the scrapbooking process. However, if you set up a great system, it could save you oodles of time down the road.

"Why bother? I'll remember what I used!" Sorry to break it to you friend, but you won't. My mind is too full of appointments for the kids, mac and cheese, to-do lists *and* whatever layout

I'm currently working on! There is just no room to remember where that piece of tape and ribbon came from.

Fear not, I have an easy technique that will have you organized in a snap: a spreadsheet. Spreadsheets (Google Docs or Excel) make me incredibly happy.

I use them to plot out everything in my digital world, including my supply lists.

Above is a part of my current credits-list spreadsheet created using Google Docs, which is conveniently located within my email account with Google.

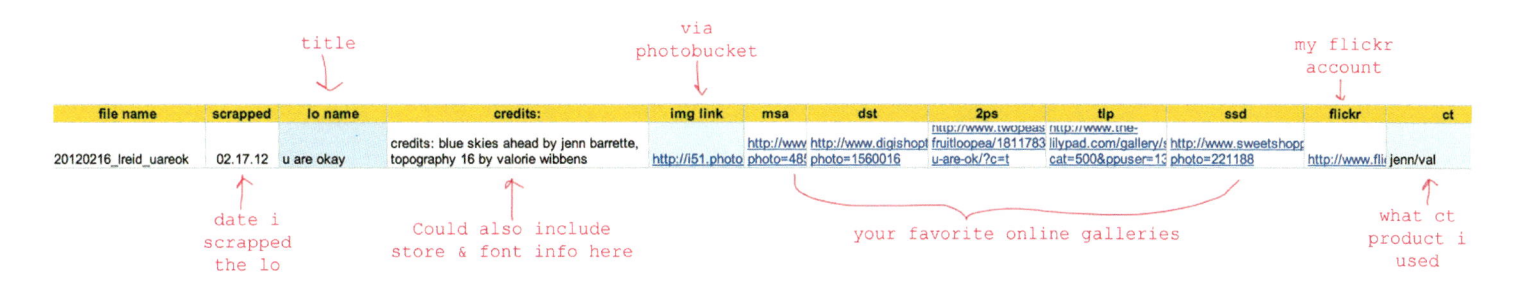

How the System Works

1 Supplies

After I complete a layout, I open my spreadsheet and start filling in the boxes. Note that I'm a digital scrapbooker.

- *File Name*: I label my pages with the date the photo was taken, my name and the title.
- *Scrapped*: I note the day I scrapped the page.
- *LO Name*: Title of the page.
- *Credits*: Here's where I put in all the nitty-gritty details. You can also include shop names and fonts.
- *CT*: The creative team for which I made the page.

2 Duplicate

Next, I upload my page to Photobucket and put that image link on my spreadsheet. Then, it's off to the galleries! I use the data from my spreadsheet to quickly cut and paste my credits list during the upload process. Then, I grab the link to my layout in each gallery and add that to my spreadsheet so I can use all this data to easily post to my creative team boards, tracking what I've scrapped for each of them.

Project Credits

6 7 | JOURNAL BY KATIE CLEMONS: JOY TO THE WORLD CHRISTMAS JOURNAL, WWW.GADANKE.COM. RED PEN: STABILO 0.4. SCRAP PAPERS, TAPE AND STICKER: FROM GERMANY.

Capturing Moments

10 | EVERYDAY STORIES: LITTLE PORTRAITS OF OUR LIFE BY CRYSTAL LIVESAY. CREDITS: DIGITAL KITS: VIOLET, SARA GLEASON; NARRATIVE, ONE LITTLE BIRD. MODERN DATES, ONE LITTLE BIRD. FONT: OLD TYPEWRITER.

20 | THE GLANCE BY BETSY SAMMARCO. SUPPLIES: CARDSTOCK: BAZZILL. PATTERNED PAPER: BASIC GREY. DIECUT FRAMES: HEIDI SWAPP. CONCHOS: SCRAPWORKS. TITLE FONT: BLUECAKE.

21 | TOTALLY IMPOSSIBLE BY BETSY SAMMARCO. SUPPLIES: DIE-CUT CARDSTOCK: KI MEMORIES. PATTERNED PAPER: PLAYDATE, JENNI BOWLIN STUDIO; HOMESPUN; BE OUR GUEST. JOURNALING CARDS: JENNI BOWLIN STUDIO / JESSICA SPRAGUE DIGITAL. STICKER: JENNI BOWLIN STUDIO. PUNCHES: JENNI BOWLIN/FISKARS BLUE RIBBON PUNCH. CUTTING FILE: SILHOUETTE TORN PAPER, JENNI BOWLIN. OTHER SUPPLIES: BAKER'S TWINE. FONTS: MOM'S TYPEWRITER, AT MODERN TWENTY.

22-23 | 1) PRESIDENT BY SARA GLEASON: DIGITAL SUPPLIES: KIT: POPS, ALLISON PENNINGTON. FONTS: 1942 REPORT, COURIER NEW. 2) BECAUSE I SAID SO BY SARA GLEASON: DIGITAL SUPPLIES: PAPERS AND WORD STRIPS: MOMSPEAK, ONE LITTLE BIRD DESIGNS. STITCHES: STITCHED BY ANNA 5, ANNA ASPNES. FONT: COURIER NEW. 3) BUGGA THANKS BY SARA GLEASON: DIGITAL SUPPLIES: VARIOUS ARTISTS.

24 | SASSY SWEET BY RENEE PEARSON. DIGITAL SUPPLIES: PAPERS: DESIGN HOUSE DIGITAL THIS WEEK AND TWENTY TWENTY, KARLA DUDLEY. BRUSHES: DESIGN HOUSE DIGITAL DIGI ESSENTIALS BRUSHES 9, STAMP SHEET (GIRL) AND REMARKABLE, KARLA DUDLEY. BUTTERFLY ELEMENT: DESIGN HOUSE DIGITAL TWENTY TWENTY, KARLA DUDLEY. JOURNALING POCKET: DESIGN HOUSE DIGITAL PROTECTOR POCKETS, KARLA DUDLEY. TEMPLATE: DESIGN HOUSE DIGITAL LIFE TEMPLATES, KARLA DUDLEY.

Telling Stories

28 | BETCHA DIDN'T KNOW BY KRISTIN RUTTEN. DIGITAL SUPPLIES: TEMPLATE: LAYERED MEMORIES NO. 50, MICHELLE MARTIN. KITS: MOSS SCAPE, MINDY TERASAWA; LITTLE ARTIST, JENNIFER BARRETTE. EMBELLISHMENTS: LITTLE FLIP-FLOPS, LIFTED WINGS NO. 1, DATE TAGS NO. 2 AND COLOR CHALLENGE FREEBIE 31509, KATIE PERTIET ; STITCHED BY ANNA - WHITE NO. 2, ANNA ASPNES. FONTS: FFF TUSJ, TRAVELING TYPEWRITER, KRISTIN'S HANDWRITING.

29 | 10K, BEFORE & AFTER BY KRISTIN RUTTEN. DIGITAL SUPPLIES: KIT: FITNESS EMBELLISHMENT BIGGIE, BRANDY MURRY. FONT: CENTURY GOTHIC.

30 | FACELESS BY CHERYL ASHCRAFT. SUPPLIES: THE GOOD WIFE BY ALISSA JONES; SOLO ACT NO. 3 BY FIZZY POP DESIGNS. FONTS: CENTURY GOTHIC AND LIKE FONTS IN THE RAIN.

31 | IT'S WHAT I LOVE TO DO! BY CHERYL ASHCRAFT. SUPPLIES: WHAT I LOVE TO DO BY STUDIO TANGIE AND STUDIO RE KNEIPP. FONT: HIGHLAND PERK. PHOTO SELF-PORTRAIT BY CHERYL ASHCRAFT.

DOCUMENTING EVERY DAY! BY CHERYL ASHCRAFT. SUPPLIES: 365 WITH YOU, BOUTIQUE CUTE DOLLS AND JULIANA KNEIPP; FUSS FREE: SET EIGHT, FIDDLE-DEE-DEE DESIGNS. FONT: TIMES NEW ROMAN. PHOTO SELF-PORTRAIT BY CHERYL ASHCRAFT.

DIGITAL DIVA BY CHERYL ASHCRAFT. SUPPLIES: MILLIE ART DOLL COLLECTION, FIDDLETTE DESIGNS; KITSCHY KREATIVE KOOL FRAMES, FIDDLETTE DESIGNS; QUEEN OF SCRAP, THE SCRAP MATTERS DESIGN TEAM; THE BRIGHT SIDE, BRITT-ISH DESIGNS; BABY BEE GARDEN, STUDIO LORIE; LUV SONG ALPHA, CD MUCKOSKY. FONT: WENDY SUE. PHOTO, OLIVIA ASHCRAFT.

32 | I STAY FLY BY TRACI REED. SUPPLIES: DIGITAL KIT: BOY CRAZY, DANI MOGSTAD. ALPHA: MODEST KRAFT ALPHA PACK, SHAWNA CLINGERMAN. TEMPLATE: JANET PHILLIPS. FONT: MRS. WEBSTER, DARCY BALDWIN.

33 | PLANNER DOWNLOAD: HTTP://ARIANSSTUDIO.BLOGSPOT.COM/2010/01/FREE-WEEKLY-PLANNER_14.HTML.

34 | G BY AMBER RIES. DIGITAL SUPPLIES: PAPERS: POTPOURRI PAPERIE PIECES, ANNA ASPNES; KEY TO MY HEART PAPERS, SAHLIN STUDIO; PRACTICALLY PERFECT, SAHLIN STUDIO AND JU KNEIPP. WASHI TAPE: WASHI TAPE 2, SAHLIN STUDIO. ALPHA: WORN SCUFFED CHIPBOARD ALPHA, SAHLIN STUDIO. DATE STAMP: EST. DATE, SAHLIN STUDIO. LACE, HEARTS, FLOWER, RIBBON, KEY, FRAMES AND TICKET STUB: KEY TO MY HEART EMBELLISHMENTS, SAHLIN STUDIO. PAINT: KEY TO MY HEART EMBELLISHMENTS, SAHLIN STUDIO; SNOWY OVERLAYS, ANNA ASPNES. TRANSFERS: ORIGINAL FOTOBLENDZ CLIPPING MASKS NO. 6, ANNA ASPNES. TORN EDGE: EASY TORN EDGES NO. 2, ANNA ASPNES. FONT: PEA ROBYN.

36 | WHY I BLOG BY CHRISTINE NEWMAN. DIGITAL SUPPLIES: DIGITAL SCRAPBOOKING KIT: TIME CAPSULE, ONE LITTLE BIRD. LETTER ALPHABETS: VINTAGE GLASS ALPHA, ONE LITTLE BIRD. FONTS: MRS BLACKFORT, SLING.

37 | MIXTAPE BY CHRISTINE NEWMAN. DIGITAL SUPPLIES: DIGITAL SCRAPBOOKING KIT: MIXED TAPE, PAISLEY PRESS. PAINT STROKES: BRUSH STROKES II: EDGES, MICHELLE COLEMAN. FONT: NEON 80S.

FEBRUARY 2012 BY CHRISTINE NEWMAN. DIGITAL SUPPLIES: MONTH STAMP: DAYS + MONTHS HAND DRAWN BRUSHES, ALI EDWARDS. SOFTWARE: ADOBE LIGHTROOM. FONTS: IMPACT, CLAIRE HAND.

38-39 | THESE ARE MY WISHES FOR YOU BY ELLE PRICE. SUPPLIES: PAPER: DENIM, AMERICAN CRAFTS; ON THE BRIGHT SIDE STITCHED AND ON THE BRIGHT SIDE POLKA, MY MIND'S EYE. LETTERS: CLASSIC CALICO COLLECTION VOL. 1 CARDSTOCK STICKERS - WHITE, STUDIO CALICO; AMY TANGERINE GOODNESS WHITE PRINTED CHIP THICKERS, AMERICAN CRAFTS. JOURNALING AND EMBELLISHMENT TAGS: LIL' SNIPPETS - THIS WEEK (GRAY), ELLE'S STUDIO; MAKE A LIST 3 X 4 JOURNALING TAGS, LIL' SNIPPET; DATE BOARDER STICKERS: CRATE STORY TELLER. EMBELLISHMENTS: GOOSEBUMPS LIME GREEN, QUEEN & CO.; CRATE TOY BOX CHIPBOARD PIECES. MIST: MISTER HUEY'S WHITE, STUDIO CALICO.

40 | THOSE EYES BY HEATHER PRINS. DIGITAL SUPPLIES: FIND MY WAY OVERLAYS, ANNA ASPNES: COASTAL KIT, SACKED SOLIDS AND BANNER STRIPS NO. 3, KATIE PERTIET.

41 | SLIPPING BY HEATHER PRINS. DIGITAL SUPPLIES: ARTPLAY PALETTE EVERYDAY, ARTPLAY PALETTE AUTUMNAL, ARTPLAY PALETTE SCHOLARLY, ARTPLAY PALETTE SMOOCH, ARTPLAY PALETTE FRIENDS, ARTPLAY PALETTE SAFFRON VILLA, FOTOGLOWS 2 AND REMEMBER WORD ART, ANNA ASPNES; YESTERDAY AND TODAY CLASS WEEK 6 WORD ART, DAY IN THE LIFE WORD ART AND GRATITUDE WORD ART FREEBIE, ALI EDWARDS.

42-43 | BEST BY JENNIFER S. WILSON. SUPPLIES: SKETCH: SIMPLE SCRAPPER PREMIUM MEMBERSHIP. CARDSTOCK: BAZZILL. PATTERNED PAPER: SUNSHINE BROADCAST GOLDEN HOUR, SASSAFRAS. EMBELLISHMENTS: BUTTONS AND FLOWERSACK: FARMHOUSE, OCTOBER AFTERNOON; CHIPBOARD PIECE: KRAFT FUNDAY, MY MIND'S EYE. LETTER STICKERS: MINI MARKET, OCTOBER AFTERNOON; AMERICAN CRAFTS THICKERS. MIST: MISTER HUEY SUNSHINE, STUDIO CALICO.

BIG LITTLE ONE BY JENNIFER S. WILSON. SUPPLIES: SKETCH: SIMPLE SCRAPPER PREMIUM MEMBERSHIP. INSPIRATION: DESIGN WORKSHOP BOOK, ELLA PUBLISHING. CARDSTOCK: BAZZILL. PATTERNED PAPER: OCTOBER AFTERNOON. STAMPS: HERO ARTS, TECHNIQUE TUESDAY, WE R MEMORY KEEPERS. EMBELLISHMENTS: AUTHENTIQUE, FANCY PANTS, OCTOBER AFTERNOON. LETTER STICKERS: AMERICAN CRAFTS. INK: STUDIO CALICO, TSUKINEKO.

EASTER BY JENNIFER S. WILSON. SUPPLIES: SKETCH: SIMPLE SCRAPPER PREMIUM MEMBERSHIP. CARDSTOCK: BAZZILL. PAPERS: COTTON TAIL, WE R MEMORY KEEPERS; REMINISCE UNWRITTEN, WE R MEMORY KEEPERS. LETTER STICKERS: AUTHENTIQUE, AMERICAN CRAFTS. PUNCH: MARTHA STEWART. STAMPS: WE R MEMORY KEEPERS. INK: TSUKINEKO VERSAMAGIC.

TEXAS BY JENNIFER S. WILSON. SUPPLIES: SKETCH: SIMPLE SCRAPPER PREMIUM MEMBERSHIP. CARDSTOCK: BAZZILL. PAPERS: BOARDING PASS NEW YORK, OCTOBER AFTERNOON; WANDER EMBARK, BASIC GREY; PANORAMA LEDGER PALM TREE, MAKING MEMORIES; ROUNDABOUT, STUDIO CALICO; ODDS AND ENDS ECLECTIC, COSMO CRICKET. LETTER STICKERS: AMERICAN CRAFTS. EMBELLISHMENTS: BUTTERFLY AND WORD TAG: FARMHOUSE, OCTOBER AFTERNOON; CHAP BADGE: AMERICAN CRAFTS; CLOCK: THE GIRLS PAPERIE; STICKY NOTE: STUDIO CALICO. PAPER TAPE: BELLA BLVD.

44-45 | THINK BIG BY CD MUCKOSKY. SUPPLIES: ALPHABET STAMPS AND METAL HARDWARE: STAMPIN' UP. OWL RUB-ON: HAMBLY. WHITE PAINT PEN: SHARPIE. FINE-TIP BLACK PEN: UNI-BALL. GLASS BEAD GEL: GOLDEN. ADHESIVE: AILEEN'S TACKY GLUE. CHIPBOARD ALPHABETS: MISCELLANEOUS. WATERCOLOR PAINTS: PRANG. MISCELLANEOUS: FABRIC, STRETCHED CANVAS, BOX TOP, PHONE BOOK PAGES, EMBROIDERY FLOSS, SHIPPING TAG, PENCIL SHAVINGS, ACRYLIC PAINT.

45 | ALL ABOUT THE TUTU BY CD MUCKOSKY. SUPPLIES: PAPER AND WIRE: MAKING MEMORIES. DOTTED PAPER FLOWERS: PRIMA. FINE-TIP PEN: UNIBALL. BLACK AND WHITE MARKERS: SHARPIE. ADHESIVE: AILEEN'S TACKY GLUE. ALCOHOL INK: TIM HOLTZ. MISCELLANEOUS:

45 (cont.) | MASKING TAPE, SCOTCH TAPE, EMBROIDERY FLOSS, BEADS, VELLUM, ACRYLIC PAINT, BOTTLE TOP, SCREW, BUBBLE WRAP, CLEAR GLITTER, TULLE FABRIC.

WHAT A GUY BY CD MUCKOSKY. SUPPLIES: BLACK PEN: UNIBALL VISION. WHITE PAINT PEN: SHARPIE. ADHESIVE: AILEEN'S TACKY GLUE. PHOTO PRINTER: HP PHOTOSMART. MISCELLANEOUS: BOX TOP, BOOT LACE, EMBROIDERY FLOSS, CORK, ACRYLIC PAINTS.

Creating Memories

48-49 | FIRST CHERRY BLOSSOM BY MELISSA STINSON. SUPPLIES: PAPERS, DIE CUTS, STICKERS, CHIPBOARD: PAPER HEART COLLECTION, CRATE PAPER. LETTER STICKERS: DIE CUT ALPHA STICKERS, STUDIO CALICO: ELM THICKERS, AMERICAN CRAFTS. MIST: MISTER HUEY CALICO WHITE, STUDIO CALICO. DOILY: CRAFT SUPPLY. PEN: UNIBALL SIGNO WHITE. DATE STAMP: OFFICE SUPPLY. INK: TSUKINEKO STAZ-ON JET BLACK.

52-53 | RIDING WITH DOGS BY JENN SMITH-SLOANE. SUPPLIES: SKETCH: DESIGNS BY ASHLEY ROCK (HTTP://WWW.DESIGNSBYASHLEYROCK.COM), REPRINTED WITH PERMISSION. PAPERS: AUTHENTIQUE BLISSFUL HAPPINESS: AUTHENTIQUE BLISSFULL PARADISE; BAZZILL BASICS LEMON BLISS; BAZZILL BASICS RAVEN; BAZZILL BASICS BLUSH RED MEDIUM; MAKING MEMORIES LEDGER. LETTER STICKERS: CHRISTMAS GLITTER DEAR LIZZY THICKERS, AMERICAN CRAFTS; LIME TWIST FLY A KITE ALPHABET STICKERS, MY MIND'S EYE. TWINE: THE TWINERY. PUNCH: DIAMOND LACE EDGE PUNCH, EK SUCCESS. PAINT AND INK: MAKING MEMORIES AND LETRASET MARKERS. OTHER EMBELLISHMENTS: STASH.

54 | STORYLAND BY PAULA GILARDE. SUPPLIES: CARDSTOCK: JILLIBEAN SOUP KRAFT CARDSTOCK. PATTERNED PAPER: JILLIBEAN SOUP OLD WORLD CABBAGE STEW. CARDSTOCK STICKERS: JILLIBEAN SOUP OLD WORLD CABBAGE STEW. LETTER STICKERS: JILLIBEAN SOUP ALPHABEANS. DIGITAL SUPPLIES: DIGITAL PHOTO CLUSTER NO. 16 BY KATIE PERTIET (DESIGNER DIGITALS).

55 | PHOTO CLUSTERS NO. 33 BY KATIE PERTIET.; CAUGHT ON FILM BY KATIE PERTIET (DESIGNER DIGITALS).

THANKSGIVING BY PAULA GILARDE. SUPPLIES: PATTERNED PAPER: JILLIBEAN SOUP APPLE CHEDDAR SOUP. CARDSTOCK STICKERS: JILLIBEAN SOUP APPLE CHEDDAR SOUP. DIGITAL SUPPLIES: CAUGHT ON FILM LAYERED TEMPLATE BY KATIE PERTIET (DESIGNER DIGITALS).

56 | FIRST MOVIE BY NANCY NALLY. SUPPLIES: CARDSTOCK: BAZZILL KRAFT. DIE: TICKET STRIP SIZZLET, TIM HOLTZ ALTERATIONS FOR SIZZIX. PATTERNED PAPER: STATIONERY OATMEAL, LILY BEE; CHARMING, AUTHENTIQUE DELIGHTFUL; PEBBLES HIP HIP HOORAY Ń CHEERS; DEAR LIZZY NEAPOLITAN - HEART SONG, AMERICAN CRAFTS; FRESH SQUEEZED-RASPBERRY JAM, AMERICAN CRAFTS. INK: TIM HOLTZ DISTRESS INK PAD IN BLACK SOOT, WALNUT STAIN, AND PUMICE STONE, RANGER. STAMPS: STAMPER'S ANONYMOUS TIM HOLTZ ODDS & ENDS; HERO ARTS NEWSPAPER BACKGROUND; TODAY YOU, TECHNIQUE TUESDAY ALI EDWARDS; THIS ONE, TECHNIQUE TUESDAY ALI EDWARDS. ALPHABET: CUPBOARD PLACARD ARMARIO, AMERICAN CRAFTS. STICKERS: DAISY GLOSSARY, MARTHA STEWART. PEN: FABER CASTELL PITT ARTIST BLACK-S.

Credits Continued

57 | JANUARY 2012 TAG BY NANCY NALLY. SUPPLIES: PATTERNED PAPER: SPRING JUBILEE COLLAGE CARDS, PINK PAISLEE; ECHO PARK HAPPY DAYS 6X6 PAPER PAD; LILY BEE HEAD OVER HEELS N SMITTEN. CARDSTOCK: CORE'DINATIONS, TIM HOLTZ KRAFT CORE NOSTALGIC COLLECTION. DIES: TAG & BOOKPLATES, SIZZIX ALTERATIONS BY TIM HOLTZ; MOVERS & SHAPERS MINI BUTTERFLIES, SIZZIX ALTERATIONS BY TIM HOLTZ. PUNCH: MARTHA STEWART CRAFTS DOILY LACE BORDER. TEMPLATE: THE CRAFTER'S WORKSHOP MINI DAMASK. STAMPS: A DAY TO REMEMBER, TECHNIQUE TUESDAY. PAINT: MARTHA STEWART CRAFTS MOTHER OF PEARL ACRYLIC PEARL CRAFT PAINT. INK: TIM HOLTZ DISTRESS BLACK SOOT INK PAD, RANGER. NUMBER STICKERS: LILY BEE PICKET FENCE ALPHABET. STICKERS: AVERY MARTHA STEWART FILE FOLDER LABELS, TIM HOLTZ IDEA-OLOGY CHIT CHAT. RHINESTONES: MARK RICHARDS HOT PINK 3MM. BRADS: FOLLOW YOUR HEART BE HAPPY, MY MIND'S EYE. PINWHEEL: PEBBLES PINWHEEL FLAGS. RIBBON: CELEBRATE IT WEDDING TULLE, MICHAEL'S.

58 | THANKSGIVING MOMENTS BY DEBBIE HODGE. SUPPLIES: DIGITAL KITS AND ELEMENTS: OAK TREE, SARAH GLEASON; AUTUMN MOON ELEMENTS, SAHLIN STUDIOS; JOURNEY BACK, VINNIE PEARCE. FONT: PEA OLSON.

59 | GUY LESSONS BY DEBBIE HODGE. SUPPLIES: DIGITAL KITS AND ELEMENTS: ARTPLAY CHEVRON CRAZY LIFE, ARTPLAY CHEVRON GIRL CRAZE, ARTPLAY ENGLISH ROSE, ANNA ASPNES; RED AND BLACK, BUTTERFLY RUBONS, JENNI BOWLIN; RIMMED FRAMERS, KRAFTY CANVAS, KATIE PERTIET; KINGDOMS PAST, TANGIE BAXTER; ARCHITECTURAL, ARTYPANTS; NARRATIVE, ONE LITTLE BIRD; BRAD BONANZA NO. 3, PATTIE KNOX; KITSCHY CHRISTMAS, SAHLIN STUDIO. FONTS: BEBAS NEUE, TRAVELING TYPEWRITER.

FRIENDS ARE A GREAT REMEDY BY DEBBIE HODGE. SUPPLIES: DIGITAL KITS AND ELEMENTS: DOUBLE TAKES, GREATEST CURIOSITY GESSO 3, ATC TANGERINE DREAMS, VINTAGE AD WORDS, TANGIE BAXTER; GENERATIONS, ONE LITTLE BIRD; SCISSORED CHEVRON, ARTPLAY CHEVRON CRAZY LIFE, MOD GRUNGE FOTOBLENDZ, ANNA ASPNES; POSTCARD JOURNALERS, OLD TIME CHRISTMAS 2, OISELET ROUGE ELEMENTS, KATIE PERTIET; JUST ANOTHER DAY, KAREN LEWIS; RELOCATE ALPHA, VIVA ARTISTRY; AUTUMN MOON ELEMENTS, SAHLIN STUDIOS; SWEET NOTHINGS ALPHA, LISA SISNEROS; IN A WORD 2, PATTIE KNOX; STITCH MEDLEY, QUIRKY TWERP.

FEED THE BIRDS BY DEBBIE HODGE. SUPPLIES: DIGITAL KITS AND ELEMENTS: OH JOY, PAISLEE PRESS; SWEETEST VICTORIA, PAULA KESSELRING; STITCHED BY ANNA WHITE, ANNA ASPNES; BETWEEN THE LINES ALPHA, KATIE PERTIET; GREATEST CURIOSITY GESSO, TANGIE BAXTER; SWEET STORYTELLER, SAHLIN STUDIO. FONTS: PRESTIGE ELITE STD, PACIFICA.

EMBROIDER ME ON YOUR PILLOW BY DEBBIE HODGE. SUPPLIES: DIGITAL KITS AND ELEMENTS: SWEET STORYTELLING, SAHLIN STUDIO; FLAIR BOX 3, POPUP STUDIO BRUSHES, PAULA KESSELRING; ANTOINNETTE, SHANNON HEGARTY; STITCH MEDLEY, QUIRKY TWERP; PURE HAPPINESS, DESIGNS BY ANITA;

59 (CONT.) | JUST LINENS 1, MAPLEBROOK STUDIO; ETC., POLKA DOT PIXELS; WESTCHESTER, ONE LITTLE BIRD; HOMESPUN STITCHES, KITSCHY DIGITALS; STORYTELLING ALPHA 2, AMANDA HEIMANN. FONTS: FELIX TITLING, JANE AUSTEN, TRAVELING TYPEWRITER.

60-61 | HAPPY. BY ANNA ASPNES. SUPPLIES: ARTPLAY PALETTES CRAZY LIFE, ARTPLAY PALETTE SUN FUN, PAINTEDHEARTS NO. 2 BRUSHSET, ANNA ASPNES; FONT IS ALL HAIL JULIA.

62-63 | SEEMS LIKE YESTERDAY BY CINDY LIEBEL. SUPPLIES: PATTERNED PAPER: CREATIVE MEMORIES. EMBOSSED POLKA DOT CARDSTOCK: CREATIVE MEMORIES. TEXTURED CARDSTOCK: AMERICAN CRAFTS. PEARLS AND JEWELS: DOODLEBUG. LABELS: ELLE'S STUDIO. KRAFT ENVELOPE & TAG: MAYA ROAD. LETTER STICKERS: LILY BEE DESIGN. TOOLS: CAMEO (SILHOUETTE): LIFESTYLE CRAFTS. WOOD GRAIN EMBOSSING FOLDER: PROVO CRAFT. CIRCLE MAKER: CREATIVE MEMORIES. TINY BUTTERFLY PUNCH: FISKARS. SMALL BUTTERFLY PUNCH: EK SUCCESS. SCALLOP BORDER PUNCH: FISKARS. DUAL-TIP ARCHIVAL PEN: CREATIVE MEMORIES. PREMIUM GLOSSY PHOTO PAPER: EPSON, INC.

64 | BIRTHDAY GIRL BY ROBYN MEIEROTTO. SUPPLIES: DIGITAL PAPERS: HAPPY DAY, ROBYN MEIEROTTO; SPRINKLES ON TOP, ROBYN MEIEROTTO; SWEET BEE, JEN ALLYSON. CARDSTOCK: BAZZILL; EPSON ULTRA PREMIUM PRESENTATION PAPER MATTE. DIGITAL ELEMENTS: HELLO MY NAME IS CARD: COUNTY FAIR, GENNIFER BURSETT; HAPPY HAPPY FLAG: SWEET BEE, JEN ALLYSON; PAINT SPLATTER: PAINT SPLATTERS-SET ONE, ERICA COOMBS. OTHER SUPPLIES: GLASSINE BAG: PRETTY TAPE, ETSY; MUSLIN RIBBON: (MIST)ABLES, PINK PAISLEY; FLOWER: AMY TANGERINE. TOOLS: DATE STAMP: STUDIO CALICO FEBRUARY KIT; LETTER STAMPS: STAPLES; PUNCH: SWISS CHEESE LARGE EDGER PUNCH, EK. SOFTWARE: PHOTOSHOP CS4 OTHER: NUMBER STICKER, DOILIES.

65 | SERIOUSLY? BY ROBYN MEIEROTTO. SUPPLIES: DIGITAL PAPERS: LET'S GO, ROBYN MEIEROTTO. CARDSTOCK: BAZZILL; EPSON ULTRA PREMIUM PRESENTATION PAPER MATTE. DIGITAL ELEMENTS: WORDS: SIMPLY SAID, GENNIFER BURSETT; NUMBERS: CURRENTLY: THE ELEMENTS, AUDREY NEAL; LOVE LOVE LOVE ELEMENTS: ROBYN MEIEROTTO. OTHER SUPPLIES: TAPE: LEBOXBOUTIQUE, ETSY; TICKET: MY MIND'S EYE KRAFT FUNDAY. TOOLS: DATE STAMP: STAPLES. SOFTWARE: PHOTOSHOP CS4.

67 | LIFE MOVES PRETTY FAST BY MICHELLE HERNANDEZ. SUPPLIES: BACKGROUND PAPERS: STUDIO CALICO AND BASIC GREY. PAPER LAYERS: GAUCHE ALCHEMY. PEG STAMPS: EK SUCCESS AND HERO ARTS. BUTTONS: PRIMA AND CRATE PAPER. OTHER SUPPLIES: BRAD: GIRLS PAPERIE; LETTER STICKERS: COSMO CRICKET; TAPE: EK SUCCESS; ARROW STICKERS: EK SUCCESS; STAPLES: TIM HOLTZ; KRAFT TAGS AND HEART: GAUCHE ALCHEMY.

68-69 | HERE COMES THE SUN BY AMY KINGSFORD. SUPPLIES: PAPERS: SEI FIELD NOTES COLLECTION, SEI DESERT SPRINGS COLLECTION, SEI VANILLA SUNSHINE COLLECTION. EMBELLISHMENTS: SEI VANILLA SUNSHINE DIE-CUT PACK. ALPHAS: SEI BLACK LICORICE PUFF ALPHABET, SEI VANILLA SUNSHINE ALPHA STICKERS. OTHER SUPPLIES: STENCILS: AVERY. BRADS: SEI VANILLA SUNSHINE SUNDRIES, BASIC GREY OUT OF PRINT, MY MIND'S EYE LOST AND FOUND. ADHESIVES: SEI GREEN WASHI TAPE, 3M FOAM SQUARES AND SCOTCH ATG GUN.

69 | TREE HUGGER BY AMY KINGSFORD. SUPPLIES: PAPERS: SEI DESERT SPRINGS TEXTURED CARDSTOCK BLUE. EMBELLISHMENTS: SEI VANILLA SUNSHINE DIE-CUT PACK, SEI VANILLA SUNSHINE SUNDRIES, SEI VANILLA SUNSHINE 3-D STICKERS, MARTHA STEWART'S CRYSTAL GLITTER. ALPHAS: SEI PUFF ALPHABET GREEN, SEI CARDBOARD ALPHA. ADHESIVES: SEI WASHI TAPE GREEN, LIQUITEX CLEAR GLOSS GEL AND SCOTCH ATG GUN. OTHER SUPPLIES: CLOUD STENCIL (MANUFACTURER UNKNOWN), BLACK SHARPIE PAINT PEN AND PAINT BRUSH.

70 | MY PAWPAW BY ASHLI OLIVER. SUPPLIES: PAPERS: OCTOBER AFTERNOON SASPARILLA. LETTER STICKERS: MARQUISE THICKERS, AMERICAN CRAFTS. PAINT: SALVAGED HOUSE PAINT. PENS: FABER CASTELL/DESIGN MEMORY CRAFTS BLACK "B" PITT PEN; UNI BALL SIGNO GEL PEN. LABEL SPOTS: JILLIBEAN SOUP. EMBELLISHMENTS: OCTOBER AFTERNOON SASPARILLA FLOWER STACK. MIST: STUDIO CALICO MISTER HUEY'S CALICO WHITE.

71 | HEY PRETTY GIRL! BY ASHLI OLIVER. SUPPLIES: PAPERS. HEAD OVER HEELS, LILYBEE; BASIC GREY BASICS WHITE. LETTER STICKERS: DEAR LIZZY NEAPOLITAN BLACK SPLENDID THICKERS, AMERICAN CRAFTS. TWINE: DIVINE TINE BLACK LICORICE. FLOWER BRAD: PEBBLES. WASHI TAPE: BLACK DOT SMASH TAPE, K & COMPANY. WATERCOLOR PENCILS: FABER CASTELL/DESIGN MEMORY CRAFT AQUARELLE PENCILS. PENS: FABER CASTELL/DESIGN MEMORY CRAFTS BLACK "B" PITT PEN; UNI BALL SIGNO GEL PEN; ZIG PLATINUM PEN. STICKERS: HEAD OVER HEELS, LILYBEE . MIST: STUDIO CALICO MISTER HUEY'S CLAY.

SISTERS & FRIENDS BY ASHLI OLIVER. SUPPLIES: PAPERS: FOLLOW YOUR HEART, MY MIND'S EYE. LETTER STICKERS: ROOTEBEAR FLOAT FOAM THICKERS, AMERICAN CRAFTS; HAPPILY LOST ALPHA STICKERS, LILYBEE. ART MEDIUM: LIQUITEX ACRYLIC MATTE MEDIUM. TWINE: DIVINE TINE BLACK LICORICE. FLOWER BRAD: PEBBLES. WASHI TAPE: BLACK DOT SMASH TAPE, K & COMPANY. PUNCH: GRANDMA'S DOILY, JENNI BOWLIN FOR FISKARS. PENS: ZIG PLATINUM. CHIPBOARD SHAPE: FOLLOW YOUR HEART, MY MIND'S EYE. MIST: STUDIO CALICO MISTER HUEY'S CLAY.

MAKE A WISH! BY ASHLI OLIVER. SUPPLIES: PAPERS: KISSING BOOTH, BASIC GREY. LETTER STICKERS: DOLL FABRIC THICKERS, AMERICAN CRAFTS. WASHI TAPE: BLACK DOT SMASH TAPE, K & COMPANY; BLACK FLORAL, HAMBLY. PENCILS: FABER CASTELL/DESIGN MEMORY CRAFT AQUARELLE PENCILS. PENS: FABER CASTELL/DESIGN MEMORY CRAFTS BLACK "B" PITT PEN. ART MEDIUM: LIQUITEX ACRYLIC MATTE MEDIUM. STICKERS: KISSING BOOTH, BASIC GREY. STAMP: POLKA DOT CLING STAMP, HERO ARTS. MIST: STUDIO CALICO MISTER HUEY'S CLOVER, INDIA INK.

72 | 1) LET'S GO TO LIMA BY AMY TAN. SUPPLIES: AMY TANGERINE DAYBOOK, FABRIC PAPER AND DIE CUT, OFFICE SUPPLY TAG, STAMP FROM JAPAN, HERO ARTS INK. 2) AMAZING CATACOMBS BY AMY TAN. SUPPLIES: PEBBLES, STUDIO CALICO, AMY TANGERINE. 3) NO WAY BY AMY TAN. SUPPLIES: MT WASHI TAPE, STUDIO CALICO, AMY TANGERINE WASHI TAPE, MY LITTLE SHOEBOX.

74 | MINI BOOKS BY ELISE CRIPE. SUPPLIES: PAPER: AMERICAN CRAFTS AMY TANGERINE. LETTER STICKERS: AMERICAN CRAFTS AMY TANGERINE.

75 | 1) PALM SPRINGS MINI BOOK BY ELISE CRIPE. SUPPLIES: CARDSTOCK: PAPER SOURCE. PAPERS: JILLIBEAN SOUP, MY MIND'S EYE, ECHO PARK PAPER CO. FONT: BEAD CHAIN. 2) NYC MINI BOOK BY ELISE CRIPE. SUPPLIES: PAPER: AMERICAN CRAFTS AMY TANGERINE. 3) HAWAII MINI ALBUM BY ELISE CRIPE. SUPPLIES: TAGS: OFFICE DEPOT. STAMP: OFFICE DEPOT. INK: STAZ-ON.

76 | U ARE OKAY BY LAUREN REID. SUPPLIES: DIGITAL KITS: BLUE SKIES AHEAD, JENN BARRETTE; TOPOGRAPHY 16, VALORIE WIBBENS.

Contributor Websites

Cheryl Ashcraft - fiddle-dee-deedesigns.com
Anna Aspnes - annaaspnesdesigns.com
Katie Clemons - makingthishome.com
Elise Blaha Cripe - eliseblaha.typepad.com
Paula Gilarde - paulagilarde.com
Sara Gleason - plantyourstory.com
Michelle Hernandez - myanaloglife.blogspot.com
Debbie Hodge - getitscrapped.com
Katrina Kennedy - captureyour365.com
Amy Kingsford - amykingsford.com
Cindy Liebel - tctliebel.typepad.com
Crystal Livesay - liveyourstories.com
Angie Lucas - angielucas.com
Robyn Meierotto - pinktrikedesign.com
CD Muckosky - cdmuckosky.com
Nancy Nally - scrapbookupdate.com
Christine Newman - listgirl.com
Ashli Oliver - purplemailbox.com
Amanda Padgett - everydayelementsonline.com
Renee Pearson - reneepearson.com
Elle Price - shopellesstudio.com
Heather Prins - heatherprins.wordpress.com
Traci Reed - tracireed.com
Lauren Reid - onestorydown.com
Amber Ries - zaubera.blogspot.com
Kristin Rutten - logyourmemory.com
Betsy Sammarco - justapharmgirl.blogspot.com
Jenn Smith-Sloane - liveteachcreate.com
Jessica Sprague - jessicasprague.com
Melissa Stinson - scrappyjedi.com
Amy Tan - amytangerine.com
Tiffany Tillman - simplytiffanystudios.com
Jennifer S. Wilson - simplescrapper.com

Sponsor Websites

Thank you to our launch party sponsors:
Anna Aspnes Designs - annaaspnesdesigns.com
Big Picture Classes - bigpictureclasses.com
Capture Your 365 - captureyour365.com
Elise Joy - elisejoy.etsy.com
Elle's Studio - shopellesstudio.com
Everyday Elements - everydayelementsonline.com
Get it Scrapped - getitscrapped.com
Jenni Bowlin Studio Mercantile - jbsmercantile.com
Jessica Sprague - jessicasprague.com
One Story Down - onestorydown.com
Paperclipping - paperclipping.com
Renee Pearson - reneepearson.com
Scrap Orchard - scraporchard.com
Simon Says Stamp - simonsaysstamp.com